Reading and Writing for Today's Adults

Voyager

7

Ted Knight

Advisers to the Series

Mary Dunn Siedow
Director
North Carolina Literacy Resource Center
Raleigh, NC

Linda Thistlethwaite
Associate Director
The Central Illinois Adult Education Service Center
Western Illinois University
Macomb, IL

Reviewer

Patricia Huelsman
Adult Basic Education
Waubonsee Community College
Aurora, IL

New Readers Press

Acknowledgments

Angelou, Maya. From *I Know Why the Caged Bird Sings* by Maya Angelou. Copyright © 1969 by Maya Angelou. Reprinted by permission of Random House, Inc. and Virago Press.

Cohen, Michael. From *The Twenty-Something American Dream* by Michael Cohen. Copyright © 1993 by Michael Cohen. Used by permission of Dutton Signet, a division of Penguin Books USA Inc.

Fulghum, Robert. "A Different Kind of Cinderella Story" from *Uh-Oh* by Robert Fulghum. Copyright © 1991 by Robert Fulghum. Reprinted by permission of Villard Books, a division of Random House, Inc. and HarperCollins Publishers, Ltd.

Fulghum, Robert. "A Modern Cinderella Story" from *Uh-Oh* by Robert Fulghum. Copyright © 1991 by Robert Fulghum. Reprinted by permission of Villard Books, a division of Random House, Inc. and HarperCollins Publishers, Ltd.

Gomez, Jeff. Reprinted with the permission of Scribner, a Division of Simon & Schuster from *Our Noise* by Jeff Gomez. Copyright © 1995 by Jeff Gomez. Also reprinted by permission of ICM International Creative Management, Inc.

Grodin, Charles. "Jobs and Money" from *How I Get Through Life* by Charles Grodin. Copyright © 1992 by Charles Grodin. Reprinted by permission of William Morrow & Company, Inc. and The Robert Lantz-Joy Harris Literary Agency, Inc.

Hughes, Langston. From *Selected Poems* by Langston Hughes. Copyright 1926 by Alfred A. Knopf, Inc. and renewed 1954 by Langston Hughes. Reprinted by permission of the Alfred A. Knopf and Harold Ober Associates.

Kleiman, Carol. "Yes, You Can Get That Raise" by Carol Kleiman. Reprinted with permission from the December 1995 Reader's Digest. Used with permission from *The Career Coach*. © 1994 by Carol Kleiman. Published by Dearborn Financial Publishing, Inc./Chicago. All rights reserved.

Kriegel, Robert J. Reprinted by permission of Warner Books, Inc. NY from *If It Ain't Broke . . . Break It!* by Robert J. Kriegel with Louis Patler. Copyright © 1990 by Robert J. Kriegel. All rights reserved.

Kuralt, Charles. "The Free Doctor" by Charles Kuralt. Reprinted by permission of The Putnam Publishing Group from *On the Road with Charles Kuralt* by Charles Kuralt. Copyright © 1985 by Charles Kuralt.

Kuralt, Charles. "The Pilot" by Charles Kuralt. Reprinted by permission of The Putnam Publishing Group from *On the Road with Charles Kuralt* by Charles Kuralt. Copyright © 1985 by Charles Kuralt.

Mazie, David. "Robot Helper" excerpted with permission from "Where It Pays to Have a Great Idea" by David Mazie, *Reader's Digest*, June 1995. Copyright © 1995 by the Reader's Digest Assn., Inc.

Miller, Annetta. "A Sensible Guide to Risk Taking," from "The Big T(hrill) Personality" by Annetta Miller as appeared in *Working Woman* Magazine. February 1990. Reprinted by permission of the author.

Raybon, Patricia. "Letting in Light" by Patricia Raybon, *The New York Times Sunday Magazine*, February 21, 1993. Copyright © 1993 by The New York Times Co. Reprinted by permission.

Ridgway, Peggi. From *Jump-Start Your Job Search* by Peggi Ridgway, Wordpictures, 1994. Reprinted with permission.

Rivas, Bimbo. "A Job" by Bimbo Rivas from *Aloud: Voices from the Nuyorican Poets Cafe* edited by Miguel Algarin and Bob Holman.

Rooney, Andrew. From *Not That You Asked . . .* by Andy Rooney. Copyright © 1989 by Essay Productions, Inc. Reprinted by permission of Random House, Inc.

Rosellini, Lynn. From "Our Century" by Lynn Rosellini, *U.S. News & World Report*. Copyright, Aug. 28/Sept. 4, 1995 U.S. News & World Report. Reprinted by permission.

Simon, Neil. From *The Prisoner of Second Avenue* by Neil Simon. Copyright © 1972 by Neil Simon. Reprinted by permission of Random House, Inc. Professionals and amateurs are warned that this play is fully protected under copyright and is subject to royalty. All rights are strictly reserved and no further rights can be exercised or used without written permission from the copyright holders.

Slack, Charles. "A Job Nobody Wanted" from "My Way Up" by Charles Slack, *Reader's Digest*, April 1995. Reprinted by permission of the author.

Swados, Harvey. "Joe, The Vanishing American" by Harvey Swados. This abridgement is an excerpt from *On the Line* originally published by Little, Brown and Company. Copyright 1957 by Harvey Swados. Copyright renewed 1985. Used by permission of Bette Swados.

Waugh, Charisse. "Work With Dignity" by Charisse Waugh, Family Circle, April 2, 1996. Reprinted with permission of *Family Circle* magazine. © 1996 by Gruner + Jahr USA Publishing.

Voyager: Reading and Writing for Today's Adults™ Voyager 7
ISBN 1-56420-157-0
Copyright © 1999
New Readers Press
U.S. Publishing Division of Laubach Literacy International
Box 131, Syracuse, New York 13210-0131

Printed in the United States of America
9 8 7 6 5 4 3

Director of Acquisitions and Development: Christina Jagger
Content Editor: Mary Hutchison
Developer: Learning Unlimited, Oak Park, IL
Developmental Editor: Pamela Bliss
Contributing Writer: Betsy Rubin
Production Director: Jennifer Lohr
Cover Design: Gerald Russell
Designer: Kimbrly Koennecke
Artist/Illustrator: Patricia A. Rapple
Copy Editor: Judi Lauber

Contents

Introduction

Welcome to New Readers Press's *Voyager 7*. In this book, you will build your reading, writing, listening, and speaking skills. You will work with familiar types of reading selections, such as essays, articles, poems, and excerpts from novels and plays. You will also work with charts and graphs.

This book has four units. Each unit is based on a theme that reflects our day-to-day lives. In *Voyager 7,* you will explore these themes:
- ▶ Getting Ahead
- ▶ Hard Times
- ▶ Then and Now
- ▶ Taking Chances

Within each theme-based unit, you will find three lessons. Each lesson has the following features:
- ▶ **Before You Read:** information and an activity to help you prepare for the reading selection, including instructions on previewing the selection and a strategy to use while reading it
- ▶ **Reading:** an essay, an excerpt from a novel or play, a poem, an article, or a graph
- ▶ **Revisit Your Strategy:** an activity that helps you judge whether you used a reading strategy effectively
- ▶ **After You Read:** questions and activities about the reading
- ▶ **Think About It:** practice with a skill that will help you understand, apply, or analyze what you read
- ▶ **Write About It:** an activity to improve your writing skills

In the back of this book, you will find an Answer Key that contains answers for Revisit Your Strategy, After You Read, and Think About It, plus the Unit Reviews. Following that is a Reference Handbook, which contains information from the Writing Skills Mini-Lesson in each unit and other useful information, including an outline of the writing process.

We hope you enjoy exploring the themes and mastering the skills found in *Voyager 7.* We also invite you to continue your studies with the last book in our series, *Voyager 8.*

Skills Preview

This Skills Preview will give you an idea about the kinds of readings and skills covered in this book. Before you begin Unit 1, please complete the entire preview. Then share your work with your instructor.

Reading Skills Preview

Read each passage and answer the questions that follow.

At 17, Greg Calhoun was living in a Montgomery, Alabama, housing project and supporting his family on the wages of a supermarket clerk. A lesson he learned from his father helped him change his life.

A Job Nobody Wanted

Charles Slack

When I turned 12, I worked summers at my father's small brick-cleaning business in Montgomery. I remember the harsh, acid smell of the cleaning solution, the scraping sound of stiff iron brushes against rough brick, and the summer sun beating down on my back. It was tempting to hurry a job just to finish, but anybody who worked for Thomas Calhoun had to meet his standards—and that included me.

If I messed up, he made me stay late until I got it right. My father wasn't being mean—he demanded the same of himself. Every brick he cleaned on a house or building stood out like a red jewel in a white setting—it was his signature.

In 1970, when I was 17, I got married and moved out of my parents' modest place into a housing project. Drugs and gang violence were just beginning to plague the projects. Friends I grew up with were soon heading in the wrong direction. Some went to jail; some were killed.

My wife, Verlyn, was 15, and nobody gave our marriage a chance. But we believed in each other, and our faith made us strong.

When we married, I had just been promoted from bagger to stock clerk at Southwest Super Foods. It was hard, tedious work. Each Friday night a truck pulled up to the store with cases of food that had to be unloaded, priced and placed on shelves, can by can and box by box. Most of the stock clerks tried to get Friday night off, but I was always ready to work.

By Saturday morning, all the cans and jars in my aisle were placed with the labels facing smartly out, like a line of soldiers on review. That was *my* signature. The floors were swept; the shelves were dusted. I took pride in a job nobody wanted.

Quit wasting your time! my friends kept saying. They assumed I wasn't going anywhere in life and that I was just a sucker.

By the 1980s, after working at several stores and rising to stock manager and beyond, I joined Hudson-Thompson Co., a grocery chain. In 1983 the company sent me to manage one of their un-profitable stores. It was Southwest Super Foods—

the very store where I'd started as a bagger 16 years earlier.

Still, I dreamed of an even bigger challenge. Within a year Verlyn and I gathered up every penny we had saved—about $35,000—got a bank loan, and persuaded the company to sell the store to me.

As owner I let employees know I was willing to pay for good work by raising everyone's salary. Then we targeted advertising to both white and black shoppers. Soon a store that had been losing $300,000 a year was making money.

With this success, Verlyn and I began looking around for other stores. Today we own eight with total revenues of $52 million a year.

With each store we've added, we make sure not to forget the details that make us successful. Each Thursday, for example, I visit one of my stores and stand in my old spot, bagging groceries.

My supervisors along the way told me that if I worked hard, I would get the chance to move up. Young people have learned to scoff at this notion, to think they're just being exploited. I knew better.

My father taught me an important lesson with an iron brush and a bucket of cleaning solution under a hot Alabama sun: each job is like a signature, and your name is only as good as the quality of work that you do.

Choose the best answer to each question.

1. Which quotation from the article best states the main idea of "A Job Nobody Wanted"?
   (1) "anybody who worked for Thomas Calhoun had to meet his standards—and that included me."
   (2) "nobody gave our marriage a chance. But we believed in each other, and our faith made us strong."
   (3) "my friends . . . assumed I wasn't going anywhere in life and that I was just a sucker."
   (4) "each job is like a signature, and your name is only as good as the quality of work that you do."

2. Greg Calhoun can be described as all of the following *except*
   (1) greedy
   (2) hard-working
   (3) ambitious
   (4) proud

3. Which detail directly supports the main idea of "A Job Nobody Wanted"?
   (1) "I remember the harsh, acid smell of the cleaning solution."
   (2) "In 1970, when I was 17, I got married and moved out of my parents' modest place."
   (3) "Drugs and gang violence were just beginning to plague the projects."
   (4) "all the cans and jars in my aisle were placed with the labels facing smartly out."

4. Why did Greg Calhoun's first store go from losing money to making money?
   (1) He always returned to the store to bag groceries.
   (2) He paid good workers well and advertised to white and black shoppers.
   (3) Both he and his wife supervised the employees carefully.
   (4) His bank loan enabled him to remodel the store.

TV journalist Charles Kuralt traveled the U.S. recording interviews
with people he found interesting. In the selection that follows,
the words spoken by Kuralt provide background information for the images
on the TV screen. Dialogue from the interview begins with
the speaker's name in capital letters. The italic text in brackets
tells what was happening at certain times in the broadcast.

The Free Doctor *(Lincoln, Missouri)*

Charles Kuralt

KURALT: It's not quite sunup yet in Lincoln, Missouri, but there's already a light in the window of Calamity Jane's Antique Shop, and the old store is full of people. They come early and take a number and take a seat. They're all waiting to see the doctor. To keep his expenses down, Dr. Richard T. Nuckles rents a little room in the back of Calamity Jane's. Here in these plain surroundings, he treats his neighbors' ailments. And he collects his fees.

DOCTOR: Okeydoke . . . three dollars all told.

KURALT: Three dollars, all told. Dr. Nuckles is not a high-priced doctor.

WOMAN: How much?

DOCTOR: One dollar. Plenty. Thank you. . . . Okay, a dollar.

KURALT: Dr. Nuckles charges you only for the medicine he dispenses. If he figures you can't afford it, then he doesn't charge you anything.

MAN: Sometimes we give him a tip, we get bighearted and give him a tip. [*Laughs*] Buy him a cup of coffee—

SECOND MAN: We feel ashamed.

MAN: Yeah—yeah, just kind of feel ashamed.

KURALT: The doctor's fee is a dollar or two. Or three at the most. We're used to doctors on their way to becoming millionaires. I told Dr. Nuckles that I hardly knew what to make of him.

DOCTOR: I'm not in it for the money—I tell 'em I expect I could have been a millionaire long as I've practiced, if I wanted to. But I didn't want to. I ain't trying to be somebody good, I'm just trying to help my fellow man.

KURALT: Much of his small income doesn't even go into the bank. It goes into the icebox. He is paid in buttermilk, and butter.

DOCTOR: Oh, my gracious, look at that. Boy! That looks good. What is it?

WOMAN: It's apple strudel—

DOCTOR: Apple strudel—

WOMAN: Without any sugar in it.

KURALT: He is paid in apple strudel, and in the deep affection of people he has known and tended to all his life.

DOCTOR: I'll work on that all right. [*Laughs*]

WOMAN: I'll bring you some more next time.

DOCTOR: Thank you.

KURALT: [*to doctor*]: Do you get a lot of produce?

DOCTOR: A lot of produce—I get everything. Fish, rabbit . . . quail, duck, wild turkey, coon . . . gooseberries, blackberries, pecans . . . chicken—all of it, and I love it. It's better than what you could buy. I'd rather have it than money!

KURALT: Dr. Nuckles does more than practice medicine. He doctors people. There's a difference.

DOCTOR: Pitting edema, pressure edema, they call it.

MAN: This leg is all right.

DOCTOR: Not as bad, no. When it's just in one leg, that shows it's not a general condition like your heart or your kidneys. If it was, it'd be both.

KURALT: Richard T. Nuckles follows in the tradition of his father, who was a country doctor, and his uncle, who was a country doctor. We are all grateful for modern medicine, and grateful for modern doctors; we're less haunted by illness because of them. But still we feel the loss of men like Richard Nuckles. Back when America was a baby, bouncing west in the lap of history, it was doctors like Doc Nuckles who saw us through our fevers and set our broken bones and held our hands. They got, in payment, only what we could give. And they always gave more than they got. It's still that way in Lincoln, Missouri.

DOCTOR: I may not get all of you picked up, but I'll pick up part of you. . . . Now—I felt a few of 'em turn loose in there—

KURALT: Complicated cases he may send to the hospital in Sedalia. But if you don't really need an operation, this doctor never recommends one.

DOCTOR: —And he's got some enlarged tonsils, and as he gets older, he won't have near as much trouble with 'em anyway, and I sure wouldn't take 'em out. He needs 'em. I think he needs 'em.

KURALT: For this advice, since it was to do nothing, he charged nothing. Dr. Nuckles rents Calamity Jane's back room—she's really Jane Neeley—for seven dollars and fifty cents a week. Jane Neeley knows how much his patients need him.

JANE: This whole area is mostly retired people, and they're on a fixed income and everything keeps going up and up—

KURALT: Everything but doctors' fees.

JANE: Well, I think he lowers his. [*Laughs*]

KURALT: [*to doctor*]: I wonder if other doctors don't sometimes get irritated with you.

DOCTOR: I'm sure they must. I'm sure they must, and I'm surprised I haven't heard from 'em. But I haven't so far—they might be gnashing their teeth—but I don't tell them what to charge, and they can't tell me what I can charge, so there you are. [*Laughs*]

KURALT: When the waiting room is finally empty, Dr. Nuckles makes house calls. They're free, too. He's been doing this for forty-eight years, doctoring anybody who comes to him, for a dollar or two, or a mason jar of buttermilk, or a handshake of thanks. You'd think he'd be ready to hang up his black bag and sit in the sun somewhere. But he'll never do that.

DOCTOR: I don't know how to retire. I'm not a setter, I just can't set around and do nothing. I tell people that getting in a rocking chair is the worst thing they can do when they retire. If I even mention quitting out here, they just come to tears—and I don't know what they'll do when I quit. It's gonna be an awful jolt, the way some of these doctors are charging.

KURALT: How many people are there who think all the time about the needs of others? And about their own needs, not at all? Well, here is one.

Choose the best answer to each question.

5. What tone does Kuralt take as he speaks about Dr. Nuckles?
(1) objective
(2) humorous
(3) admiring
(4) disbelieving

6. Based on their dialogue, what kind of relationship does Dr. Nuckles seem to have with his patients?
(1) friendly and informal, as equals
(2) authoritative and formal, like a traditional doctor-patient relationship
(3) businesslike and official, like a businessman and his customers
(4) fatherly yet controlling, like a stern father to his children

7. The setting of the interview involves each of the following *except*
(1) a doctor's office
(2) the back room of an antique shop
(3) a time when the country was young
(4) a small town in Missouri

8. From this excerpt, we can infer that Dr. Nuckles is
(1) elderly
(2) out of touch
(3) ambitious
(4) selfish

The graph below shows changes in wages and salaries of three groups of workers. It compares the percent increases for each group over a four-year period. Study the graph and answer the questions that follow.

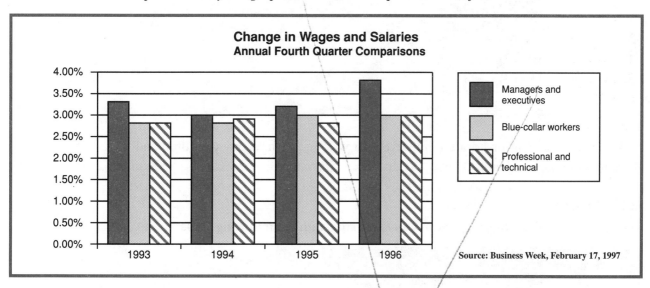

Choose the best answer to each question.

9. In what years did two categories of workers show the same percentage of change in wages and salaries?
   (1) 1993 and 1994   (3) 1994 and 1996
   (2) 1994 and 1995   (4) 1993 and 1996

10. In what year did wages and salaries of professional and technical workers increase more than those of blue-collar workers?
   (1) 1993   (3) 1995
   (2) 1994   (4) 1996

11. Which statement is a good conclusion to draw from this graph?
   (1) From 1993 through 1996, no worker earned a raise higher than 4 percent.
   (2) During this period, the salaries of managers and executives increased more than the salaries of blue-collar workers or professional and technical workers.
   (3) Business and industry had a profitable year in 1996.
   (4) Professional and technical workers merit very small raises.

Write About It

On separate paper, write about the topic below. Then use the Revising Checklist to revise your draft.

Topic: What does getting ahead mean to you? What will it take for you to get ahead? Write three or more paragraphs. Support your opinion with reasons and examples.

Revising Checklist
Revise your draft. Check that your draft
   _____ clearly states your opinion
   _____ includes reasons to support your opinion
   _____ includes details or examples to explain your reasons

Skills Preview Answers

Reading Skills Preview

1. (4)	**7.** (3)
2. (1)	**8.** (1)
3. (4)	**9.** (4)
4. (2)	**10.** (2)
5. (3)	**11.** (2)
6. (1)	

Write About It

Make changes on your first draft to improve your writing. Then recopy your draft and share it with your instructor.

Skills Chart

The questions in the Skills Preview assess familiarity with the following skills:

Question	Skill
1	Identify the main idea
2	Understand characterization
3	Identify main ideas and details
4	Understand cause and effect
5	Identify tone
6	Analyze dialogue
7	Analyze setting
8	Make inferences
9	Compare and contrast
10	Compare and contrast
11	Draw conclusions

Unit 1 Getting Ahead

People dream of getting ahead. To most people in the United States, that means having the basic necessities of food, clothing, and a home, plus steady improvement in the way they live from year to year. All that takes money, so people need jobs that pay enough. For many people, getting ahead also includes the satisfaction and sense of achievement that come from having a good job.

What does getting ahead mean to you? You have already made an important step in trying to get ahead— you are furthering your education. In this unit, you will read how one woman turned her life around. You will study graphs that compare common ways to find jobs. And you will read an article with advice on how to get raises and promotions in the quest to get ahead.

▶ **Be an Active Reader**

As you read each selection in this unit
- Put a question mark (?) by things you do not understand.
- Underline words you do not know. Try to use context clues to figure them out.

After you read each selection in this unit
- Reread sections you marked with a question mark. If they still do not make sense, discuss them with a partner or your instructor.
- Look at words you underlined. Discuss any words you still don't know the meaning of with a partner or your instructor, or look them up in a dictionary.

Lesson 1

LEARNING GOALS

Strategy: Empathize
Reading: Read an interview
Skill: Understand cause-and-effect chains
Writing: Write an action plan

Before You Read

The selection that follows is an interview with a 25-year-old woman named Marilyn. When she was growing up, Marilyn had an alcoholic father who abused her mother. At 17, Marilyn married her high-school boyfriend, who turned out to be lazy and unfaithful. You'll read about Marilyn's struggle to get ahead after this bad start in life.

Think about some of the ways a person might get off to a bad start in life. Write a few ways here.

_____

_____

Some people manage to overcome a bad start and build successful lives. What personal qualities do you think help them do that?

_____

_____

The following selection is based on the author's interview with Marilyn. Much of what you will read are her spoken words. Think about how people speak. Listen to someone talking. Do you hear words like "gonna" and "y'know"? Words like those are in the interview. When you read the selection, read Marilyn's words as if you could hear her speaking.

Preview the Reading

Look at the illustrations. Read the first paragraph and the first line of each of the next few paragraphs. What do you think might happen with Marilyn's job search?

Set Your Strategy: Empathize

When you empathize, you identify with the thoughts, feelings, and experiences of another person. If you can empathize with people you read about, you will understand them better. As you read the following selection, try to empathize with Marilyn—put yourself in her place and feel what she must have been feeling. When you finish, you will have a chance to tell how you think she must have felt during certain incidents in her life.

*In this interview, you will read about Marilyn, a single mother,
and her experiences in getting a job and working to build a career.*

Marilyn

Michael Lee Cohen

The same day that Marilyn left her husband, she went looking for a job. A friend of hers worked for a company that manufactures heat pumps in Oklahoma City, and Marilyn's friend told her that she made almost double the minimum wage. Marilyn, who had never earned more than minimum wage and had no job skills, thought, "I could support the boys and myself on that."

"So I went up to the temporary service, and they said, 'Marilyn, you wouldn't want to work out there. You get dirty. You just wouldn't like it.' I said, 'Yes I do, I want to work out there.' And they wouldn't put me to work out there, and they called my cousin to go to work out there.

"When I went up there, I'd been like a housewife, and I had on a dress and heels and pantyhose. They said, 'Marilyn, you wouldn't like factory work. It's just—not you.' But I was ready to do anything."

Marilyn was lucky. Her cousin had just received an offer from another employer. He called Marilyn and told her that he could not accept the job at the heat pump plant and that, if she still wanted the job, she should call the people at the temporary service. So she did. She told them, "'You just called my cousin, but he's not gonna be able to report to work. But I'm ready.' And they said, 'Okay, Marilyn, you can try it.'" She reported to work later that day.

Of the 150 or so people who work on the assembly line at the heat pump plant, roughly 10 percent are women. Marilyn says, "When I first started, it felt real awkward. When we'd have breaks, the guys, they would talk about cars, and I was more into soap operas at the time. I could relate to that. And then they would talk about things, I had no idea what was going on. They talk about fishing. I'd never gone fishing before. And they'd talk about boats and mechanics and everything that guys would normally talk about. They even talked about women sometimes, when I'd be sitting there.

"A lot of people, when I first started, they used to ask me out. I'd just gotten out of my marriage. I didn't really want to have to deal with that. And I wouldn't go, like, tell anyone or anything, because I figured I could deal with it. Because sexual harassment, you get in trouble for breathing the wrong way anymore, and I didn't want to get anyone in trouble. But I did wish that they'd leave me alone so I could just work and get my job done and get my paycheck so I could go. Now I tell 'em I don't date much, and I definitely don't go out with people I work with. 'Cause that's how I make my living, and the two together just don't mix.

"I really didn't have a lot of trouble adjusting to the work though, because my dad, he's always taught us how to work hard, and we've always had to work hard. So he said, 'Gonna have to work no matter what.' 'Cause we came from just a middle-class family, you have to work, 'less you're born into richness and you can lay around, and be a bum or whatever."

Although Marilyn had little trouble adapting to the work, she struggled when she first became a single mother. She says, "Just having kids and working, it just seemed like a big responsibility. And I was havin' to do it all by myself. It was real hard, a real hard adjustment."

Marilyn finally chalked up too many absences. After five months, she was fired. She and her sons have lived with Marilyn's parents since Marilyn left her husband. Her mother takes care of the children, so that is not what caused Marilyn to miss work. Marilyn admits, "I used to go out partying, and I would be sick the next day. I'd have a hangover."

During those months of nightclubbing and drinking, Marilyn began to realize she was tumbling into the same trap of low self-esteem and liquor into which her mother had fallen. Then one morning, Marilyn's older son said to her, "Mom, are you sick again?"

"And then," she says, "I just remembered what I went through, and I thought, I don't want my kids to grow up like I did. I want my kids to have the *best possible life.* And in order to do that, I have to make it happen."

Four weeks after he fired her, Marilyn called her former boss. "I'm very sorry," she said. "I was just going through something. If you give me my job back, I'll be a lot better. I'll always be there." The boss rehired Marilyn, and she returned to the assembly line.

A year later Marilyn left the heat pump manufacturer for a job as a file clerk in the reservations office of a national airline. She was laid off six months later. Once again, Marilyn asked her former employer for her old job. Once again, he allowed her to come back.

Marilyn says, "That was the hardest thing, to go back for the third time. But I had to do it because I had to support my kids." I ask whether she felt as if she had to swallow her pride, and she quips, "A lot. I felt it in my feet." She says that "anyone that can go back to work at the same establishment—for the *third* time—can do anything."

When Marilyn started working on the assembly line, she earned $4.50 an hour. Today, she makes $7.30, 60 percent more than the current minimum wage of $4.25. And she loves her job.

"I like to work fast," she explains, "and production lines are fast. And I like to have goals to climb for, and if we have a quota, that's more or less like a goal, and you can reach that goal. And it makes me feel good when I do, because it makes me feel like I've achieved something.

"The management has always been good to me. Always. My boss, my plant manager, have always been real nice. And the people I work with, my coworkers, they're real nice. I feel real involved with the people. It's more like a family out there."

But the people at the temporary agency were right about one thing. Marilyn shows me her fingernails. Her hands are clean, but the pink fingernail polish has been mostly chipped away, and there is a black semicircle of grime lodged beneath each nail. Marilyn tells me that she can never get all the dirt out from under her fingernails. She confesses, "I get dirty. I hate to get dirty." She chuckles.

Speaking quietly yet confidently, Marilyn says, "I don't always want to be just an assembly-line worker. I want to advance within the company and move up. Not only to prove to other people, but mainly prove to myself, that I can do it, y'know. That'll be the only thing that I haven't quit. I've quit school. I quit my marriage. I've always felt like a failure. But now I feel like I can—be some-one. I'm going to be someone."

Marilyn always wanted to go back to school but never did. "I was scared," she says. "I was afraid I would be a failure and I couldn't do it." But she finally overcame her fear. For the past nine months, Marilyn has spent four hours a night, four nights a week, studying heating and air-conditioning maintenance at a technical school. She is the only woman in her program, and one of only two women in the entire school. But she's accustomed to this after nearly three years of working on the assembly line.

Marilyn will graduate in a month. After that, she plans to take some classes in accounting and business management at a community college. Her goals are to learn enough about heating and air-conditioning systems and business to become a salesperson for the heat pump manufacturer, and then to go to college to become a mechanical

engineer. She anticipates that it will take at least another six years of part-time schooling to finish her degree. "But," she notes, "six years isn't any-thing compared to the rest of your life."

▶ Revisit Your Strategy: Empathize

Think carefully about the following incidents in Marilyn's life. Choose one or more descriptions from the box that you think express her feelings during each one. Then write a sentence describing what you think she felt. The first one has been done for you.

alone	higher self-esteem	uncomfortable	upset
determined	swallowed her pride	under pressure	worried

1. "The same day that Marilyn left her husband, she went looking for a job."

   She was probably upset and worried but also determined.

2. "Just having kids and working, it just seemed like a big responsibility. And I was havin' to do it all by myself. It was real hard, a real hard adjustment."

   She's worried money to support her kids. she fells under pressure

3. "That was the hardest thing, to go back for the third time. But I had to do it because I had to support my kids."

   She swallow her pride to go back work.

4. "I've quit school. I quit my marriage. I've always felt like a failure. But now I feel like I can—be someone. I'm going to be someone."

   Marilyn has higher self-esteem because she has goal.

After You Read

A. Comprehension Check

1. Why did Marilyn apply for work at the heat pump plant?
   - (1) It was near her home.
   - (2) They advertised for assembly-line workers.
   - (3) The pay was almost double the minimum wage.
   - (4) She had experience with assembly-line work.

2. Why did the temporary service first refuse to send Marilyn for the job on the assembly line?
   - (1) She wasn't dressed for factory work.
   - (2) Women weren't allowed to work there.
   - (3) Her cousin had already been given the job.
   - (4) She did poorly at the employment interview.

3. Why did Marilyn first leave her job at the heat pump plant?
   - (1) She got a better job with an airline office.
   - (2) She experienced sexual harassment.
   - (3) Her boss didn't like her.
   - (4) She was fired for too many absences.

4. How do you think Marilyn felt at the end of this interview with Mr. Cohen?
   - (1) afraid she wouldn't graduate
   - (2) confident about the future
   - (3) unsure of what she will do next
   - (4) ready to quit school again

5. Which clue tells you that Marilyn learned to deal with co-workers who asked her out?
   - (1) She wished they would leave her alone.
   - (2) She didn't want to get anyone in trouble.
   - (3) She doesn't date people she works with.
   - (4) She wouldn't tell anyone anything.

6. In the sentence "She *anticipates* that it will take at least another six years . . . to finish her degree," *anticipates* means
   - (1) knows
   - (2) doubts
   - (3) regrets
   - (4) expects

B. Read between the Lines

Check each statement below that you think Marilyn might have made. Look back at the selection for evidence to support each statement you check.

_____ 1. "If I hadn't left my husband, my life would have been completely different."

_____ 2. "I miss those days when I could go out and have a good time after work."

_____ 3. "I want to get married again."

_____ 4. "I learned the hard way how to become a good worker and a responsible mother."

_____ 5. "Work on the assembly line taught me about setting goals and working hard."

_____ 6. "It was just luck that my boss hired me back twice."

C. Think beyond the Reading

Discuss these questions with a partner.

1. Marilyn is raising two sons as a single parent. How does her experience compare with that of other single parents you know? What advice would you give her?

2. Marilyn got off to a bad start in life. What personal qualities do you think helped her get a fresh start on the road to success? Are these the same qualities you listed in Before You Read on page 14?

Think About It: Understand Cause-and-Effect Chains

The interview with Marilyn may have raised some questions in your mind: Why did she act so irresponsibly that she lost her first job? What changes did she make in herself to become successful? When you ask questions like that, you are recognizing cause-and-effect relationships. A **cause** is an event or action that makes another event or action—an **effect**—happen:

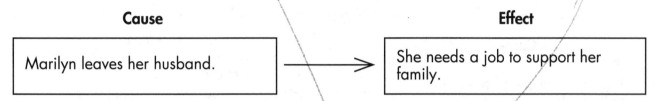

Cause	Effect
Marilyn leaves her husband.	She needs a job to support her family.

Often a cause-and-effect relationship will lead to a **cause-and-effect chain.** In a chain, the first effect becomes the cause of a second effect, and so on. Marilyn's story contains several cause-and-effect chains.

A. Look at Cause-and-Effect Chains

Reread this part of the interview with Marilyn. Notice the chain of causes and effects.

> "So I went up to the temporary service, and they said, 'Marilyn, you wouldn't want to work out there. You get dirty. You just wouldn't like it.' I said, 'Yes I do, I want to work out there.' And they wouldn't put me to work out there, and they called my cousin to go to work out there.
> "When I went up there, I'd been like a housewife, and I had on a dress and heels and pantyhose."

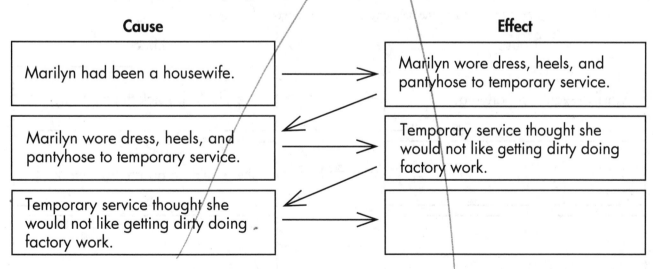

Cause	Effect
Marilyn had been a housewife.	Marilyn wore dress, heels, and pantyhose to temporary service.
Marilyn wore dress, heels, and pantyhose to temporary service.	Temporary service thought she would not like getting dirty doing factory work.
Temporary service thought she would not like getting dirty doing factory work.	

What did the temporary service do because it thought Marilyn would not like the factory job? Fill in the final effect.

If you wrote that the temporary service would not send her to work at the heat pump factory, you were correct.

B. Practice

Read each excerpt from "Marilyn." Then complete the cause-and-effect chain.

1. ▶ Marilyn was lucky. Her cousin had just received an offer from another employer. He called Marilyn and told her that . . . if she still wanted the job, she should call the people at the temporary service. So she did. She told them, "'You just called my cousin, but he's not gonna be able to report to work. But I'm ready.' And they said, 'Okay, Marilyn, you can try it.'"

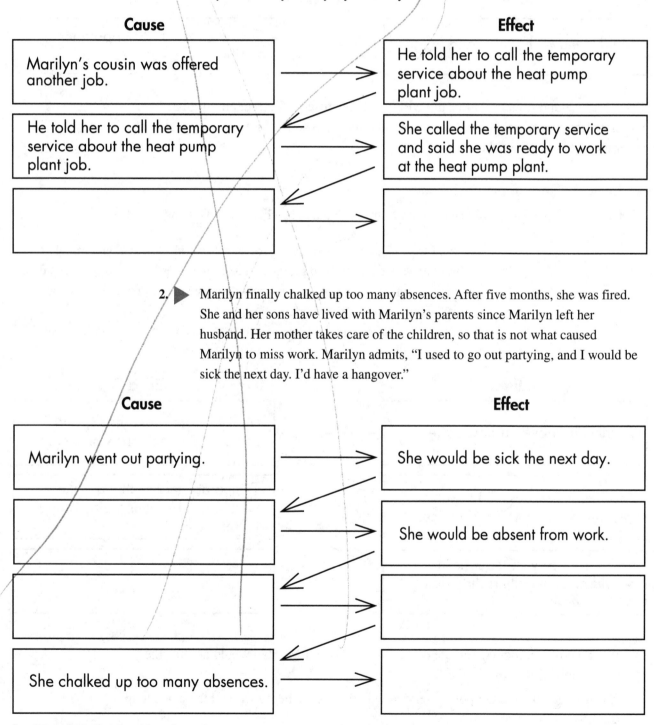

Cause

Marilyn's cousin was offered another job.

He told her to call the temporary service about the heat pump plant job.

Effect

He told her to call the temporary service about the heat pump plant job.

She called the temporary service and said she was ready to work at the heat pump plant.

2. ▶ Marilyn finally chalked up too many absences. After five months, she was fired. She and her sons have lived with Marilyn's parents since Marilyn left her husband. Her mother takes care of the children, so that is not what caused Marilyn to miss work. Marilyn admits, "I used to go out partying, and I would be sick the next day. I'd have a hangover."

Cause

Marilyn went out partying.

She chalked up too many absences.

Effect

She would be sick the next day.

She would be absent from work.

3. ▶ During those months of nightclubbing and drinking, Marilyn began to realize she was tumbling into the same trap of low self-esteem and liquor into which her mother had fallen. Then one morning, Marilyn's older son said to her, "Mom, are you sick again?"

"And then," she says, "I just remembered what I went through, and I thought, I don't want my kids to grow up like I did. I want my kids to have the *best possible life.* And in order to do that, I have to make it happen."

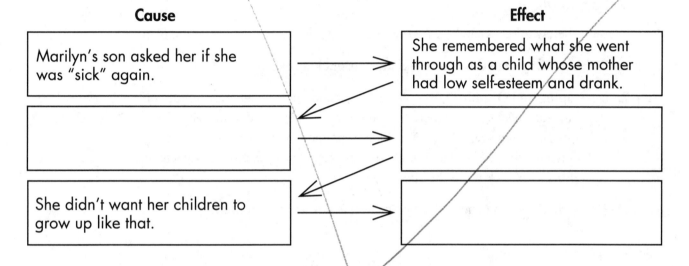

Cause

Marilyn's son asked her if she was "sick" again.

She didn't want her children to grow up like that.

Effect

She remembered what she went through as a child whose mother had low self-esteem and drank.

Tip

Be careful not to confuse events that simply happened one after the other in sequence with events that have a cause-and-effect relationship. Marilyn went to night school because she worked during the day. That is cause and effect. Marilyn went to night school and then went home. That is a sequence of events.

▶ **Talk About It**
Conduct an interview of your own with a friend, a relative, or a classmate. Prepare for the interview by writing down at least four questions. Ask what the person is doing now and what he or she would like to be doing five years from now. Take brief notes on the answers. Compare your interview results with those of another classmate.

Write About It: Write an Action Plan

In the interview with Marilyn, you saw how cause and effect can link events in a person's life. Marilyn seems to have learned how to cause positive things to happen. She has made a plan for her life that will bring positive effects. Now you will have a chance to write an action plan to achieve a goal in your own life. First, study the sample of how to write an action plan.

Study the Sample

Read the steps below to see what the writer considered as she developed her action plan.

Step 1: Picking a Goal. First she chose a goal: stop smoking.

Step 2: Developing and Organizing the Plan. Most action plans contain a number of steps that take people from where they are now to where they want to be. The writer of the sample action plan listed the steps she would take to quit smoking and numbered them. She also thought of ways to reward herself and ways to get herself back on track when she slipped.

Now read the writer's action plan on the next page. Then it will be your turn.

Your Turn

A. Prewriting

Step 1: Think about some goal that you would like to accomplish. It may be a small one, like breaking a bad habit. Or it may be a major change, like starting a new career. Choose one of the topics below, or use the list to help you think of another topic.

- break a bad habit
- lose weight
- look for a new job
- buy a car or another big item

- make some new friends
- earn your GED
- repair a damaged relationship
- learn a new skill

Write the goal for your action plan here. My goal is to _____.

Step 2: Think about the things you need to do to accomplish your goal. On separate paper, list those actions and then number them as stages and steps. Think of a way to measure your progress and a way to get back on track if you don't keep to the steps in the plan. Decide how to reward yourself for successes.

My Action Plan to Stop Smoking

Stage 1: Cut back on the number of cigarettes I smoke each day

Step 1: Limit myself to 12 cigarettes per day.
- Stop buying cartons of cigarettes.
- Stop having a cigarette after eating.
- Don't go to Step 2 until I successfully do 7 days in a row.

Step 2: Limit myself to 6 cigarettes per day.
- Smoke only during work hours.
- Don't go to Step 3 until I successfully do 7 days in a row.

Step 3: Limit myself to 3 cigarettes per day.
- Don't smoke when drinking coffee.
- Don't go to Stage 2 until I successfully do 7 days in a row.

Stage 2: Stop smoking completely

Throw away any cigarettes at home and at work.

Tell everyone that I have quit and not to offer me cigarettes.

At the end of each week without a cigarette, treat myself to dinner out and a movie.

B. Writing

On separate paper, write the first draft of your action plan. Use numbered stages and steps to go from the first step to the final result.

Tip As you write your action plan, you may think of steps to add or steps you want to drop or change. Go ahead and make these changes as you write your first draft.

▶ **Save your draft.** At the end of this unit, you will work with one of your drafts further.

Lesson 2

LEARNING GOALS

Strategy: Restate
Reading: Read a graph
Skill: Draw conclusions
Writing: Write an informative essay

Before You Read

Most adults have had to look for a job. If you haven't, you probably know someone who has. In this lesson, you will find out about methods people have used to find job openings. Which of the following job-search methods are you already familiar with?

_____ help-wanted ads   _____ contacting employers directly
_____ private employment agency   _____ union hiring hall
_____ state employment agency   _____ civil service exam
_____ asking friends   _____ asking relatives

1. List any others that you know about.

_____

_____

2. If someone asked you for advice about the best way to find a job opening, which methods would you suggest? Why?

_____

_____

Preview the Reading

Data is factual information usually expressed in numbers, for example, measurements or statistics. The job-search data in this lesson is presented in a double-bar graph. Read the title and the labels. Read the key to understand what the dark blue and light blue bars represent.

Set Your Strategy: Restate

When you restate, you put information into your own words. To restate data from a bar graph, tell in your own words what the numbers mean and how the lengths of the bars compare. As you study the following graph, try to restate data. When you finish, you will have a chance to write some of your restatements.

Researchers at the U.S. Bureau of the Census talked to 10 million people who found jobs in a single year. The survey asked what methods they used to find job openings and which one found the job they got. The graph below shows some of what the researchers learned.

The Job Search: What Works?

The double-bar graph below shows how many job seekers used each of these job search methods and how many found jobs using each one.

The horizontal axis along the bottom of the graph shows the job search methods. The vertical axis shows the number of people in millions. In each pair the dark blue bar shows how many people out of the 10 million polled tried that method. The light blue bar shows the number of people who found a job with that method. For example, about 2 million of the job seekers polled tried a private employment agency, and about 500,000 of them actually got jobs that way. A little more than 6.5 million people tried applying directly to employers, and about 3.5 million were successful.

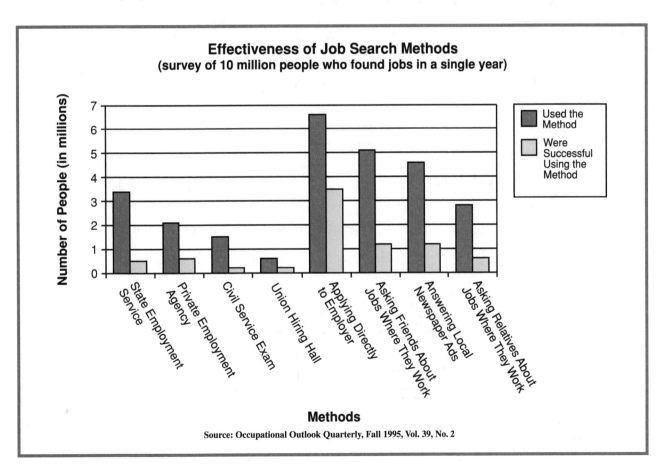

Effectiveness of Job Search Methods
(survey of 10 million people who found jobs in a single year)

Source: Occupational Outlook Quarterly, Fall 1995, Vol. 39, No. 2

You can use this graph to see how often each job-search method succeeded.

You can estimate the success rate of a method by comparing the heights of bars. Look on the graph at Applying Directly to Employer. The dark blue bar is about twice as high as the light blue bar. That means that for every 2 people who used this method, 1 person found a job. The success rate was 1 in 2.

Math can give you a more precise success rate. For example, the graph tells us that about 6.5 million people tried applying directly to an employer and about 3.5 million succeeded. 6.5 million divided by 3.5 million equals about 1.9 (or using math symbols: $6,500,000 \div 3,500,000 \approx 1.9$). This gives us a more precise success rate: 1 in 1.9.

Similarly, for Private Employment Agency on the graph, $2,000,000 \div 500,000 = 4$. Using a private employment agency had a lower success rate: 1 in 4.

Look at the bars for Civil Service Exam and answer the following questions.

1. About how many people took a civil service exam? _____

2. About how many people got a job using this method? _____

3. What is the success rate of this method? _____

About 1,500,000 people took a civil service exam. About 250,000 people got a job by that method. So the success rate was 1 in 6.

▶ **Revisit Your Strategy: Restate**

1. Look at the bars labeled Union Hiring Hall. Fill in the blanks in this restatement of the data.

   While about _____ people used a union hiring hall to find a job,

   about _____ were successful using that method. The success rate

   was about _____.

2. Based on the restatement above, restate the data in the last pair of bars.

   _____

   _____

After You Read

A. Comprehension Check

1. About how many people polled used a state employment service in their job search?
(1) 5 million   (3) 2 million
(2) 3.5 million   (4) .5 million

2. Which of the first four job search methods on the graph had the highest success rate?
(1) state employment service
(2) private employment agency
(3) civil service exam
(4) union hiring hall

3. Using a private employment agency had a success rate of about 1 in 4. What other job search method had the same rate?
(1) state employment service
(2) civil service exam
(3) applying directly to employer
(4) asking friends about jobs where they work

4. Which method was used by the most people?
(1) using a state employment service
(2) using a union hiring hall
(3) applying directly to employer
(4) answering local newspaper ads

5. What was the success rate of using a state employment service?
(1) about 1 in 3.5 million   (3) about 1 in 7
(2) about 1 in 20   (4) about 1 in 2

6. Which of the following job search methods had the lowest success rate?
(1) applying directly to employer
(2) asking friends about jobs where they work
(3) answering local newspaper ads
(4) asking relatives about jobs where they work

B. Read between the Lines

Check each statement below that can be proven correct according to the information in the graph. Be able to identify the bars on the graph that support the statements you check.

_____ **1.** There are more state employment services than there are private agencies.
_____ **2.** Many people use more than one method to look for a job.
_____ **3.** More people get jobs by asking friends and relatives than by using state and private employment agencies.
_____ **4.** Using the newspaper classified ads isn't the best way to find a job.
_____ **5.** Asking both relatives and friends will increase the chances of finding a job.
_____ **6.** You can get a job through a union hiring hall only if you belong to a union.

C. Think beyond the Reading

Think about the graphs, and discuss them with a partner. Answer the questions in writing on separate paper if you wish.

1. Why do you think applying directly to an employer is so effective in finding a job?
2. Look back at your response to question 2 in Before You Read on page 24. Based on what you learned from the graph, what advice would you give now?

Think About It: Draw Conclusions

When you **draw a conclusion,** you figure out something you have not been told directly. You can often draw conclusions from a graph. Graphs present data in an organized way. We draw conclusions from the data. For example, the graph on page 25 tells us hundreds of thousands of people got jobs using each method. You can conclude that if you are looking for a job, using several methods will increase your chances.

A. Look at Drawing Conclusions

The graph below is a circle graph. A circle graph (also called a pie chart) represents all of something—one whole. The percentages of all the sections in any circle graph will add up to 100 percent.

This circle graph, which shows data from the *Occupational Outlook Quarterly,* predicts that 2.5 million sales jobs would be created between 1994 and 2005. Each section shows the percentage of those new jobs projected for each type of sales worker. For example, the circle graph predicts that 22 percent of the new jobs will be for cashiers. That's close to one-fourth of all the jobs. You could restate that data this way: "Nearly one-fourth of all the new sales jobs will be for cashiers."

To get all you can out of the graph, however, you don't want to just restate data. You also want to draw conclusions from it.

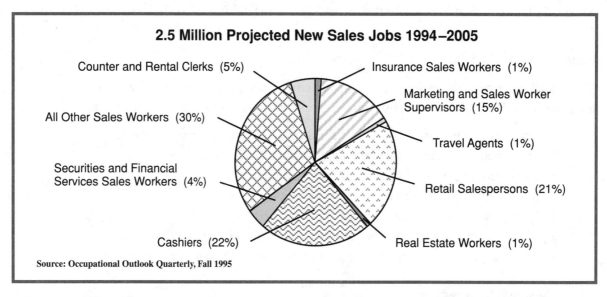

2.5 Million Projected New Sales Jobs 1994–2005

Counter and Rental Clerks (5%)
Insurance Sales Workers (1%)
Marketing and Sales Worker Supervisors (15%)
All Other Sales Workers (30%)
Travel Agents (1%)
Securities and Financial Services Sales Workers (4%)
Retail Salespersons (21%)
Cashiers (22%)
Real Estate Workers (1%)

Source: Occupational Outlook Quarterly, Fall 1995

As you study the circle graph, think of what you know about sales jobs. Then think about the data the graph presents and what you can conclude from it. Which statement below is an accurate conclusion that you can draw from the data?

_____ **1.** Stores will be the most important source of new sales jobs.
_____ **2.** One supervisor is needed for about every 6 sales workers.

You should have picked statement 1. Stores account for 43 percent of the projected new jobs—the Retail Salespersons and Cashiers categories. No data on the graph shows the relationship between supervisors and sales workers.

Tip

When you read a graph, read all the labels carefully to be sure you understand what the graph is showing. If you don't, you may not understand the information correctly, and you may draw wrong conclusions.

B. Practice

The circle graphs below show the distribution of the U.S. labor force by age. Each section of each graph represents the percentage of the labor force that is in a certain age range.

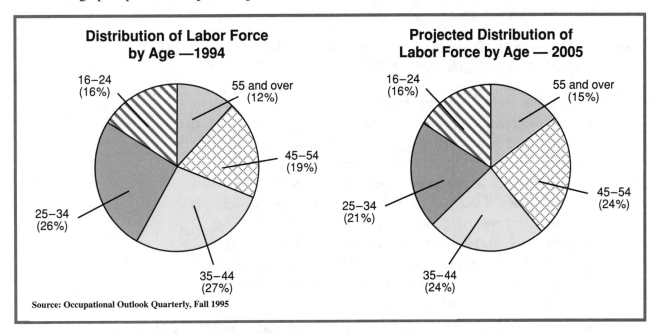

Source: Occupational Outlook Quarterly, Fall 1995

1. Study the first circle graph. Think of what you know about the labor force. Think of what you can conclude from the data. Check each conclusion you can draw.

_____ **a.** About 12 percent of people working in 1994 will have retired by 2005.
_____ **b.** Most 16-year-olds worked part time in 1994.
_____ **c.** Nearly one third of U.S. workers were at least 45 years old in 1994.

2. Study the second graph. Compare it with the first graph. Check each conclusion you can draw from the predicted changes in the labor force.

_____ **a.** The average age of workers in this country is projected to increase.
_____ **b.** There will be as many 16–24-year-olds in 2005 as in 1994.
_____ **c.** The percentage of workers aged 25–34 will decrease by the year 2005.
_____ **d.** In 2005 the labor force will be the same size as in 1994.

▶ **Talk About It**

Take a survey. Ask people what methods they used to get their jobs. List the methods and tally how many people used each one. Then make a single bar graph to show the data. Compare graphs with your classmates.

Write About It: Write an Informative Essay

In this lesson, you have been reading graphs that contain employment data. Now you will have a chance to write an informative essay about the data in an employment graph. First, study the sample.

Study the Sample

Read the steps below to see what the writer did as he developed his informative essay.

Step 1: Picking a Topic. The writer decided to write about the graph "2.5 Million Projected New Sales Jobs 1994–2005" on page 28.

Step 2: Developing and Organizing Ideas

Restate Key Ideas. The first step in getting ideas to write about is to restate the data presented in the graph. Below are restatements of key ideas for the essay about the graph "2.5 Million Projected New Sales Jobs 1994–2005":

- 2.5 million new sales jobs are expected from 1994 to 2005.
- Most of the new jobs will fall into three major kinds: cashiers, retail salespersons, and marketing and sales worker supervisors.
- Other unspecified jobs represent about a third of the growth.
- Other sales jobs experiencing growth will be counter and rental clerks, securities and financial services sales workers, insurance sales workers, real estate workers, and travel agents.

Draw Conclusions. An informative essay does more than just restate data. Here are two conclusions the writer drew from the same graph.

- Stores will be the most important source of new sales jobs.
- People with good skills in math and customer relations should consider stores as possible employers.

Now read the writer's informative essay on the next page. Then it will be your turn.

Your Turn

A. Prewriting

Step 1: Choose a graph that interests you and that you want to write about. It could be
- one of the graphs from this lesson
- a graph you find in a newspaper or magazine or on the Internet

Write the name of the graph you are going to write about on the line below.

_____

2.5 Million Projected New Sales Jobs: 1994–2005

If the growth in jobs meets projections, people who want to work in sales should consider focusing their job hunt on stores between 1994 and 2005.

According to information in *Occupational Outlook Quarterly,* 2.5 million new sales jobs will be created between 1994 and 2005. More than half of that growth will be in three specific kinds of jobs: cashiers, retail salespersons, and marketing and sales worker supervisors. Other sales jobs expected to grow include counter and rental clerks, securities and financial services sales workers, insurance sales workers, real estate workers, and travel agents. And a large portion of new sales jobs—about a third—will be in other unspecified sales jobs.

Because cashiers and retail salespersons represent such a large portion of the new jobs—43 percent of the total—stores should be one of the areas of highest growth. To qualify for jobs in stores, applicants need good skills in customer relations. And because the jobs involve handling money accurately, good math skills are also important.

People with these skills who want to work in sales should consider stores as possible employers. In that area of high growth, they would stand the best chance of finding a sales job between 1994 and 2005.

Step 2: On separate paper, restate information from the graph you chose. You don't need to restate all the data. Write the key ideas presented in the graph in your own words. Then look at your key ideas and the graph and write at least one conclusion you can draw.

B. Writing

On separate paper, write an informative essay about the graph you selected.

Tip

It's helpful to a reader if you begin your essay with an important general conclusion drawn from the graph. Use one or more middle paragraphs to show how the data supports this conclusion. Then end your essay with a statement that sums up the data.

▶ **Save your draft.** At the end of this unit, you will work with one of your drafts further.

Lesson 3

LEARNING GOALS

Strategy: Summarize
Reading: Read an informative article
Skill: Identify the main idea and details
Writing: Write a summary

Before You Read

The magazine article you are about to read offers strategies you can use to get a raise in pay. The author is an employment expert. She uses real-life examples from her clients' experiences to illustrate her points. Before you read the article, think about the following questions and write responses.

1. Have you ever asked for a raise in pay? If so, what did you say? If not, what do you think you would say?

   _____

   _____

2. How do you think a worker can know when it's a good time to ask for a raise?

   _____

   _____

3. If you are not given a raise when you ask for one, how long do you think you should wait before asking again?

   _____

As you read "Yes, You Can Get That Raise," see if you think the author would agree with your answers.

Preview the Reading

Read the five headings in bold type. Try to predict what each section will be about.

Set Your Strategy: Summarize

When you summarize, you state in your own words only the main points of a piece of writing. You can also sum up the main points with one general statement of the author's message. As you read "Yes, You Can Get That Raise," think about the main points that the author is making. Underline them, highlight them, or note them in the margin or on paper to remember them. When you finish reading the article, you will have a chance to choose a general opening statement for a summary.

Today many companies are looking for ways to cut costs and increase profits. Many employees are finding that regular pay raises are a thing of the past. In this article, an expert describes strategies you can use to ask for and get more money.

Yes, You Can Get That Raise

Carol Kleiman

Early in my career I obeyed the maxim "Don't make waves." I was the sole support of three children and had a job I loved. I feared bringing attention to myself, so I just did what I was told, stayed quiet—and missed out on important assignments.

When I finally summoned the courage to speak up, my supervisors were surprised. They simply hadn't known what I was interested in. Once I learned to ask for what I wanted, I got the opportunity to do bigger jobs.

These days you can't afford to be self-effacing[1]—especially if you want to make sure you're in line for one of the few raises and promotions that are available. Just as you marketed yourself to get the right job, now you have to continue to market yourself to be recognized as a player.

There is no one simple way to get ahead, but based on real-life experiences I hear every day as a columnist writing about employment, here are the strategies that work best:

Confront your fear and nervousness. Don't be afraid to say you are qualified to do a different job or to move ahead. An assistant hotel manager told me, "I can speak up for everyone in the department. But when it comes to what *I* want, I have a hard time saying anything." He had missed out on chances to get promoted.

Letting people know how much you'd like to help open that new hotel in

---

1. self-effacing: not drawing attention to oneself

Kauai,[2] or be the next sales manager in your department, is something you will have to work at. No one will give you the plum unless you make it clear that's what you want.

Be an "A" player. Raises used to be virtually automatic. Not anymore—if you don't perform well, you probably won't get any raise at all. The raises go to those the company considers its "A" players.

That means you have to be an eager beaver. Just as it's more than okay to work overtime when it's appropriate, it's also more than okay to be alert to other work that needs to be done. Today, being called an "eager beaver" is a compliment.

Ten years ago, when his company was looking to computerize, a human-resources assistant was asked to handle a few details of the new project. He already had plenty of work to do and computers weren't his specialty, but he accepted the assignment enthusiastically and learned all he could about the equipment.

The assistant helped the company select machines and software and then supervised computer training of the staff—including the top executives. Today his job includes not only computers, but also office space and the firm's outside real-estate holdings.

Take advantage of performance reviews. At many companies you are eligible for a raise only if you've had a review. Use the evaluation to make a pitch for a raise.

Your manager will notify you in advance of an upcoming appraisal. Then you're often given time to fill out a form that includes questions about how you rate your work, your strengths and contributions. You also get a chance to write down what you see as areas for improvement and what your career objectives are.

If you've helped complete a successful project in the past year, say so. If you've worked long hours, mentored[3] another employee or volunteered for special activities, now's the time to tell your boss.

On most evaluation forms, an important topic for discussion is "employee's career objectives." Tell your boss clearly and with conviction what you really want.

Have a backup plan. "I went into my boss's office anticipating a really good discussion. I was told that I was getting a three-percent raise. They'd try to do better next year—and that was it," an office manager said to me. "It was depressing, but there was nothing I could do."

She was right. Most raises are predetermined. Managers often have a fixed sum of money for their departments, and if they increase your raise,

---

2. Kauai (COW/eye): a Hawaiian island
3. mentored: trained or guided someone's career

they'll have to take something away from someone else. When they allocate[4] money, they usually try to bring up the salaries of those who are severely underpaid and to reward the very top performers.

If there's not much of a raise for you, make clear to your supervisor how disappointed you are. Remind him or her of the new project you completed that brought in thousands of dollars. Request another meeting in a few months to continue the discussion and to see if the company is in a better position to increase your pay.

"I thought I'd never be able to make more money," a reader told me. "I was stuck at three-percent raises each year. But at my performance reviews I kept letting my boss know how serious and ambitious I was." The payoff after five years was a ten-percent raise and a promotion.

Give yourself a raise. If you haven't gotten a good salary increase in years or you're at the top of your range, it's time to polish up your résumé and search for another job.

The first place to look is inside your own company. Most have formal job postings for openings. Try out for jobs you're interested in—whether or not you have all the qualifications.

"When I applied for the job of assistant financial manager at my company, everyone was in shock," said a sales representative at a manufacturing company. "I was doing well, but I was getting burned out. I put in for the job even though I knew I was a few credentials short."

The sales rep didn't get the job, but at least management was now aware of a motivated candidate. "I saw that what I needed was an MBA, and within a year I was accepted into the company's special graduate training program at a nearby university," the rep said. "I'm still working on my degree, and I'm still a sales rep—but I know when I complete the program, I'll be next in line for any opening in the financial department."

Applying for jobs posted is just one way of letting your employer know the important skills you possess that you haven't been able to utilize. Seize every opportunity that comes along and you'll grow into an irreplaceable asset who doesn't even have to ask for what you're worth.

---

4. allocate (A/lo/kate): distribute according to a plan

▶ **Revisit Your Strategy: Summarize**
Which of the following would be the best opening statement for a summary of "Yes, You Can Get That Raise"?
(1) You have to market yourself to be recognized as deserving a raise.
(2) To get a raise you need to overcome your fear and nervousness.
(3) There are five useful strategies for getting a raise.
(4) Seize every opportunity that comes along.

After You Read

A. Comprehension Check

1. Early in the author's career, she missed out on important assignments because
   (1) she didn't speak up
   (2) she was a single parent
   (3) she loved her job
   (4) few raises or promotions were available

2. An "A" player is an employee who
   (1) follows orders well
   (2) gets automatic raises
   (3) works in human resources
   (4) takes on extra work

3. Employees may fail to get a good raise for all the following reasons *except*
   (1) fear and nervousness
   (2) poor planning
   (3) self-marketing
   (4) limits on the money available for raises

4. The human-resources assistant was promoted because
   (1) he knew a lot about computers
   (2) he didn't have enough to do
   (3) he learned all he could about computers
   (4) he didn't like his previous job

5. In the sentence "Early in my career I obeyed the *maxim* 'Don't make waves,'" *maxim* means
   (1) a passing whim   (3) a bad habit
   (2) a rule to live by   (4) a law of nature

6. If an employee refuses to do extra work, you can infer that
   (1) she is likely to get an automatic raise
   (2) her performance review is likely to be canceled
   (3) she is likely to be transferred to another department
   (4) she is likely to miss out on raises and promotions

B. Read between the Lines

Check all the statements below that you can conclude are true based on this article.

_____ 1. You will get what you want from your employer if you just ask for it.
_____ 2. Performance reviews are used to plan for the future as well as judge past work.
_____ 3. Not getting a raise you ask for means your boss has a low opinion of your work.
_____ 4. Sometimes your only chance for earning more money is to get another job.
_____ 5. Supervisors can change their minds about what an employee is worth.
_____ 6. A good boss knows what his or her employees want without being told.

C. Think beyond the Reading

Think about the reading, and discuss it with a partner. Answer the questions in writing on separate paper if you wish.

1. Not all workers have the kind of job where they can take on a special project or mentor another employee in order to earn a raise or a promotion. What other things might a worker do to merit special attention from the boss?

2. Look again at your answer to the first question in Before You Read on page 32. Would you change what you said or would say when asking for a raise? If so, how?

Think About It: Identify the Main Ideas and Details

The **main idea** of a piece of writing is the central thought or general point of the material. **Details** are the specific facts, examples, and reasons the writer gives to support the main idea. Sometimes the main idea is stated directly by the writer. Sometimes the main idea is implied, and you have to figure it out, or infer it, based on the details the writer provides.

A piece of writing can have several levels of main ideas:
- The whole piece of writing has one overall main idea, also called the **theme.**
- If the piece of writing has sections, each section has its own main idea.
- Within each section, each paragraph can have its own main idea.

A. Look at Main Ideas and Details

Read the following paragraph from the article, and then answer the questions.

> Early in my career I obeyed the maxim "Don't make waves." I was the sole support of three children and had a job I loved. I feared bringing attention to myself, so I just did what I was told, stayed quiet—and missed out on important assignments.

1. What is the main idea of this paragraph?

_____

2. Write three facts, examples, or reasons that support this main idea.

_____

_____

_____

The main idea of the paragraph is that the author missed opportunities because she stayed quiet. To support this idea, the author offers these facts: "I obeyed the maxim 'Don't make waves,'" "I was the sole support of three children and had a job I loved," "I feared bringing attention to myself," and ". . . I did just what I was told, stayed quiet—and missed out on important assignments."

Tip Pay careful attention to the facts, examples, and reasons a writer offers as supporting details. They will help you understand a main idea that is stated. They will help you infer a main idea that is not.

B. Practice

The article is divided into five sections, each beginning with a sentence printed in **bold.**

1. Reread the section beginning "Confront your fear and nervousness." Then fill in the main idea and supporting details below.
   a. Main idea of the section:

   _____

   b. Three details—facts, examples, or reasons that support this main idea:

   _____

   _____

   _____

2. Reread the section beginning "Be an 'A' player." Then fill in the main idea and supporting details below.
   a. Main idea of the section:

   _____

   b. Three details—facts, examples, or reasons that support this main idea:

   _____

   _____

   _____

3. Reread the section beginning "Take advantage of performance reviews." Then fill in the main idea and supporting details below.
   a. Main idea of the section:

   _____

   b. Three details—facts, examples, or reasons that support this main idea:

   _____

   _____

   _____

4. Reread the section beginning "Have a backup plan." Then fill in the main idea and supporting details below.

    a. Main idea of the section:

_____

    b. Four details—facts, examples, or reasons that support this main idea:

_____

_____

_____

_____

5. Reread the section beginning "Give yourself a raise." Then fill in the main idea and supporting details below.

    a. Main idea of the section:

_____

    b. Three details—facts, examples, or reasons that support this main idea:

_____

_____

_____

▶ **Talk About It**

Discuss experiences you or someone you know has had in seeking a raise in pay or a promotion. Look for examples of successful or unsuccessful uses of each of the five strategies described in the article. Has anyone used another strategy, one the author didn't describe? Was it successful or unsuccessful? List each strategy, and briefly note who tried it and what happened.

Write About It: Write a Summary

When you summarize, you briefly retell in your own words the main ideas of an article, story, or event. In this section, you will have a chance to write a summary of the article "Yes, You Can Get That Raise." The box below lists tips for writing a good summary.

How to Summarize an Article

- Identify what the article is about in general—the author's main message.
- Identify the main ideas in the article.
- Put the ideas in your own words.

A. Prewriting

Step 1: Identify the author's main message. You did this in Revisit Your Strategy on page 35. Copy that sentence on the line below. It will make a good opening statement for your summary.

_____

Step 2: Identify the main ideas. On pages 38 and 39, you wrote a sentence that identified the main idea of each of the five sections in the article. Review the main idea you wrote for each section.
- Do you want to reword any of these statements?
- Do you want to expand any statement to explain it more clearly or thoroughly? For example, you may want to add details to help explain the main idea statement. For the first section, you could write, "First, if you want a raise or promotion, you need to overcome your nervousness, ask for it, and explain why you are qualified." If you want to make any changes to these statements, either make the changes in this book or write the new main idea sentences on paper.

B. Writing

You can summarize an article like "Yes, You Can Get That Raise" in six or seven sentences. Write the title of the article on the top line of your paper. Begin your summary with the opening statement you wrote above. Then use the statements you revised in Step 2 above to summarize the ideas in each section in your own words.

Tip To help your reader identify the main points of your summary, begin them with *First, Second, Third,* and so on.

 Save your draft. At the end of this unit, you will work with one of your drafts further.

Writing Skills Mini-Lesson: Compound Sentences

A **compound sentence** has two or more complete thoughts usually joined by one of these connecting words: *and, but, or, so,* or *yet.* To write a compound sentence, follow these rules.

1. **Make each part of the sentence a *complete thought.*** Include a **subject** (who or what the sentence is about) and a **verb** (what the subject does or is) in each part.

   S   V   S   V

   Kay loved sports, and **she wanted** to be a sportswriter.

2. **Use an appropriate connecting word.**
   - *and* for related ideas
   - *or* for choices
   - *so* for one idea that causes another
   - *but* or *yet* for contrasting ideas

3. **Use a comma before the connecting word.**
   The newspaper needed a sports reporter, **so** the editor placed an ad.
   Kay applied for the job, **and** the editor called her for an interview.
   The editor recognized Kay's talent, **but** he didn't want to hire her.
   Kay's writing sample was good, **yet** she didn't have much experience.
   Kay could walk away, **or** she could speak up for herself.

Practice

Did Kay get the newspaper job? On your own paper, combine each pair of sentences to make a compound sentence. Use a comma and an appropriate connecting word.

1. Kay liked to write about sports. She had once interviewed Michael Jordan.
2. The newspaper was looking for a sportswriter. Kay saw the ad.
3. Kay could ignore the ad. She could take the chance.
4. She really wanted the job. She applied.
5. The editor liked Kay. He didn't want to hire a woman.
6. She knows a lot about sports. The male athletes could be rude to her.
7. Kay showed the editor samples of her work. The editor read them over.
8. The editor could hire Kay. He could pass up a gifted sportswriter.
9. The editor was very impressed by Kay's work. He decided to hire her.
10. Kay took the job. She became a well-known sportswriter.
11. Kay got married. Then a few years later she had a baby.
12. Kay could stay home with the baby. She could find a good child-care center.
13. Kay thought about quitting. She loved her work and wanted to continue.
14. Her husband Fred decided to care for their child. He quit his job.
15. Now Fred is a full-time father and homemaker. He couldn't be happier.

Reading Review

In this article, actor and talk-show host Charles Grodin explains
his attitude toward work and the desire to get ahead.

Jobs and Money
(What Do People Want and Why?)

Charles Grodin

When I was eighteen years old, I saw a movie starring Elizabeth Taylor and Montgomery Clift and decided I wanted to become a movie star. It had nothing to do with a job or money. It had to do with romance. I had a crush on Elizabeth Taylor. As for acting, it was a profession in which I had no experience except for my role of Don, the janitor boy, in *Getting Gracie Graduated,* my grammar school play, but part of Montgomery Clift's genius was he made acting look easy. After a short while I realized that acting was even harder than meeting Elizabeth Taylor.

At that point I forgot about being a movie star and even Elizabeth Taylor and became fascinated with learning about the craft of acting. Still, none of this in any way felt like a job, and the subject of money to me was where did I get ten dollars a week to pay my rent.

I got my money with part-time jobs that paid for rent and acting classes. That was it. I wasn't even thinking about making a lot of money or being famous. I was only thinking about getting better at acting.

As time went by and I began to work as an actor, make money, and even achieve some fame, I still basically thought about the work, not the money or fame. As I've said, I stayed in my small apartment in New York with no stove.

It seems that then, as now, professionally I defined a work experience more by what was it like to be there than how successful it turned out. The quality of life was what it's been about. Some people that I've met and befriended for a time haven't seen it that way. They are what I think of as the careerists. Success and fame seem to outstrip all other considerations, such as human relationships. I'm sure, of course, these people inhabit every profession. The work, they tell themselves, is the thing. Everything comes after the work—friendships, family, whatever. These people even seem to take a sense of professional pride in this attitude, as though it made them a little more dedicated than their co-workers. To me it shows a desperation and an inability to sustain much interest for any period of time in anything beyond their personal advancement. These people can be bright, charming, and may even appear to be interested in you—but not really, unless you can help their careers.

They may say they do all this for their families, but their families usually just want them, not more money. Careerists bore easily if you're not talking about them or their field, and they can make you feel boring. These people can definitely be damaging to your health.

What do they want? One former friend seems to

want to be the richest person in the world. A friend of mine once said that all these money seekers should get together and live above a bank. Most of these people have no strong friendships. I remember seeing Lena Horne once on *60 Minutes* announce ruefully something to the effect of "I've had a hell of a career, but I don't have any friends."

I don't believe we choose to be the way we are in this area. As I've said, friends have always been a necessity to me. My life needs that. I can't sit in a nice home, have a good bank account, and feel warm all over. I require the love of family and friends. If offered a choice, I'll take less money and more friends. I'm grateful I'm that way, just as I'm sorry I'm some other ways.

I guess the best we can do for ourselves in this or any department is try to figure out what we really think and feel and are we happy with it. If we can answer that question, maybe what follows helps us get through life a little bit better.

Choose the best answer to each question.

1. The author first decided to become an actor when he
   (1) fell in love with an actress in a movie
   (2) saw how easy acting was
   (3) enjoyed acting in a grammar school play
   (4) realized he wanted to be famous

2. Which of the following best expresses the author's main point about himself?
   (1) "I was only thinking about getting better at acting."
   (2) "Success and fame seem to outstrip all other considerations."
   (3) "Everything comes after the work— friendships, family, whatever."
   (4) "I'll take less money and more friends."

3. The author believes he is the way he is because
   (1) he has learned from his experiences with careerists
   (2) he remembers what his family taught him
   (3) that's just the way he is—he didn't choose it
   (4) movies showed him how to be

4. Which of the following could you conclude about the author?
   (1) He chooses acting parts because they interest him.
   (2) He wishes he had made more money.
   (3) He does not have many friends.
   (4) If he could do it over again, he would choose a different career.

The graph below compares increases in wages and savings in a fictional town from 1991 through 1996.

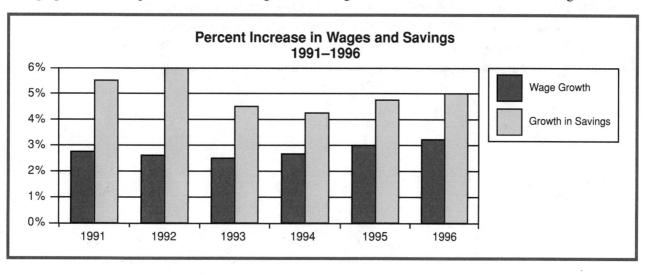

Choose the best answer to each question.

5. During which year did wage increases begin to rise after a period of decline?
(1) 1993   (3) 1995
(2) 1994   (4) 1996

6. Which of the following statements best describes the growth in savings from 1991 to 1996?
(1) gradual increase, then a sharp drop, then a gradual increase
(2) constant up-and-down shifts
(3) fairly level, staying just below or above 3 percent
(4) a sharp increase followed by a more gradual increase

7. During which year did people increase their savings most in comparison to their wages?
(1) 1991   (3) 1993
(2) 1992   (4) 1994

8. Based on this graph, what likely happened to growth in wages and savings in 1997?
(1) They increased by nearly equal percentages.
(2) Savings continued to grow, while wages remained steady.
(3) Growth in savings exceeded growth in wages.
(4) Growth in wages exceeded growth in savings.

The Writing Process

In Unit 1 you wrote three first drafts. Choose below the draft that you would like to work with further. You will revise, edit, and make a final copy of this draft.

_____ your action plan to achieve a positive goal in your life on pages 22–23
_____ your informative essay using the data from a graph on pages 30–31
_____ your summary of the article "Yes, You Can Get That Raise" on page 40

Find the first draft you chose. Then turn to page 176 in this book. Follow steps 3, 4, and 5 in the Writing Process to create a final draft.

As you revise, check your draft for these specific points.

Action plan: Are the steps listed in the order in which you will do them? Does your plan include a way to measure your progress and reward yourself when you are successful?

Informative essay: Have you clearly restated the key facts in the graph and drawn one or two conclusions from the data?

Summary: Does your summary clearly state the main idea of the article and only the main points about it?

Unit 2 Hard Times

When people are out of work, times are hard. When families don't have enough money to make ends meet, times are hard. The future is uncertain. People can become frightened, even desperate. But most people do survive hard times, and they can come through stronger than they were before. In this unit, you will read about the hard times seen by a young African American growing up in the Great Depression of the 1930s. You will read a poem about an out-of-work man searching for a job. And you will read a scene from a play about a man who may soon lose his job.

Before you begin Unit 2, think about hard times you may have had. What helped you make it through? Did your hard times make you stronger? Wiser? In what ways?

▶ **Be an Active Reader**

As you read the selections in this unit
- Put a question mark (?) by things you do not understand.
- Underline words you do not know. Try to use context clues to figure them out.

After you read each selection in this unit
- Reread sections you marked with a question mark. If they still do not make sense, discuss them with a partner or your instructor.
- Look at words you underlined. Discuss any words you still don't know the meaning of with a partner or your instructor, or look them up in a dictionary.

Lesson 4 ▶ LEARNING GOALS

Strategy: Use context clues
Reading: Read an excerpt from an autobiography
Skill: Analyze setting
Writing: Describe a setting

Before You Read

Maya Angelou is a poet, playwright, performer, and composer. She is best known, however, for several autobiographical books. The selection that follows is from the first of these books, *I Know Why the Caged Bird Sings*. This book tells of the hard times Angelou saw as an African American girl growing up in the 1930s. She was raised by her grandmother in a racially divided small town in Arkansas. Before you read the selection, think about these questions and write responses.

1. The 1930s were the time of the Great Depression. What do you know about the hard times people experienced during the Depression?

   _____

2. What do you know about the lives of African Americans living in small southern towns in the 1930s?

   _____

3. What do you think a child would notice growing up in such a community?

   _____

Preview the Reading

Look at the illustrations. What do they suggest about the reading selection? Read the introduction. What do you think the author might be going to tell you about living at her grandmother's store? Read the footnotes that define some of the words in the selection.

Set Your Strategy: Use Context Clues

When skilled readers come across an unfamiliar word in their reading, they use context clues to help them figure out the meaning of the word. Context clues are the words and sentences near a word that help explain its meaning.

In addition to the words defined in the footnotes, you may find several unfamiliar words in this reading selection. When you come to an unfamiliar word, read the words before and after it. Try to figure out its meaning by thinking of a word that would make sense in the sentence.

When Maya Angelou was three and her brother Bailey was four,
their parents divorced. The two children were sent to be raised by their grandmother,
Mrs. Annie Henderson, in Stamps, Arkansas. In the following selection,
Angelou tells of life in and around her grandmother's general store.

I Know Why the Caged Bird Sings

Maya Angelou

AP/WIDE WORLD PHOTOS

Maya Angelou

We lived with our grandmother and uncle in the rear of the Store (it was always spoken of with a capital *s*), which she had owned some twenty-five years.

Early in the century, Momma (we soon stopped calling her Grandmother) sold lunches to the sawmen in the lumberyard (east Stamps) and the seedmen at the cotton gin (west Stamps). Her crisp meat pies and cool lemonade, when joined to her miraculous ability to be in two places at the same time, assured her business success. From being a mobile lunch counter, she set up a stand between the two points of fiscal[1] interest and supplied the workers' needs for a few years. Then she had the Store built in the heart of the Negro area. Over the years it became the lay center of activities in town. On Saturdays, barbers sat their customers in the shade on the porch of the Store, and troubadours on their ceaseless crawlings through the South leaned across its benches and

---

1. fiscal: relating to money

sang their sad songs of The Brazos[2] while they played juice harps and cigar-box guitars.

The formal name of the Store was the Wm. Johnson General Merchandise Store. Customers could find food staples, a good variety of colored thread, mash for hogs, corn for chickens, coal oil for lamps, light bulbs for the wealthy, shoestrings, hair dressing, balloons, and flower seeds. Anything not visible had only to be ordered.

Until we became familiar enough to belong to the Store and it to us, we were locked up in a Fun House of Things where the attendant had gone home for life.

Each year I watched the field across from the Store turn caterpillar green, then gradually frosty white. I knew exactly how long it would be before the big wagons would pull into the front yard and load on the cotton pickers at daybreak to carry them to the remains of slavery's plantations.

During the picking season my grandmother would get out of bed at four o'clock (she never used an alarm clock) and creak down to her knees and chant in a sleep-filled voice, "Our Father, thank you for letting me see this New Day. Thank you that you didn't allow the bed I lay on last night to be my cooling board,[3] nor my blanket my winding sheet.[4] Guide my feet this day along the straight and narrow, and help me to put a bridle on my tongue. Bless this house, and everybody in it. Thank you, in the name of your Son, Jesus Christ, Amen."

Before she had quite arisen, she called our names and issued orders, and pushed her large feet into homemade slippers and across the bare lye-washed wooden floor to light the coal-oil lamp.

The lamplight in the Store gave a soft make-believe feeling to our world which made me want to whisper and walk about on tiptoe. The odors of onions and oranges and kerosene had been mixing all night and wouldn't be disturbed until the wooded slat was removed from the door and the early morning air forced its way in with the bodies of people who had walked miles to reach the pickup place.

"Sister, I'll have two cans of sardines."

"I'm gonna work so fast today I'm gonna make you look like you standing still."

"Lemme have a hunk uh cheese and some sody crackers."

"Just gimme a coupla them fat peanut paddies." That would be from a picker who was taking his lunch. The greasy brown paper sack was stuck behind the bib of his overalls. He'd use the candy as a snack before the noon sun called the workers to rest.

In those tender mornings the Store was full of laughing, joking, boasting

---

2. **Brazos (BRA/zus):** a river and territory in Texas
3. **cooling board:** a board or plank on which a dead person was laid
4. **winding sheet:** a sheet for wrapping a dead body; a shroud

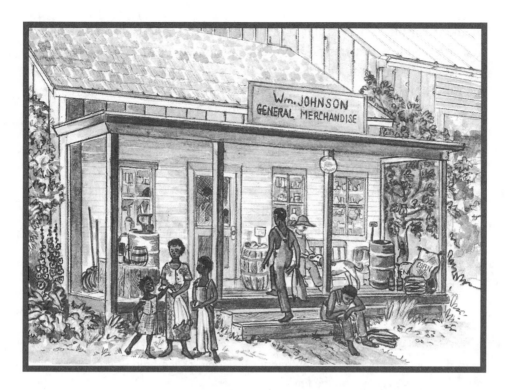

and bragging. One man was going to pick two hundred pounds of cotton, and another three hundred. Even the children were promising to bring home fo' bits and six bits[5].

The champion picker of the day before was the hero of the dawn. If he prophesied that the cotton in today's field was going to be sparse and stick to the bolls[6] like glue, every listener would grunt a hearty agreement.

The sound of the empty cotton sacks dragging over the floor and the murmurs of waking people were sliced by the cash register as we rang up the five-cent sales.

If the morning sounds and smells were touched with the supernatural, the late afternoon had all the features of the normal Arkansas life. In the dying sunlight the people dragged, rather than their empty cotton sacks.

Brought back to the Store, the pickers would step out of the backs of trucks and fold down, dirt-disappointed, to the ground. No matter how much they had picked, it wasn't enough. Their wages wouldn't even get them out of debt to my grandmother, not to mention the staggering bill that waited on them at the white commissary downtown.

The sounds of the new morning had been replaced with grumbles about cheating houses, weighted scales, snakes, skimpy cotton and dusty rows. In later years I was to confront the stereotyped picture of gay song-singing cotton pickers with such inordinate rage that I was told even by fellow Blacks that my paranoia[7] was embarrassing. But I had seen the fingers cut

---

5. fo' bits and six bits: fifty and seventy-five cents
6. boll (bole): cotton seed-pod
7. paranoia (PAR/uh/NOY/ah): great fear of persecution

by the mean little cotton bolls, and I had witnessed the backs and shoulders and arms and legs resisting any further demands.

Some of the workers would leave their sacks at the Store to be picked up the following morning, but a few had to take them home for repairs. I winced to picture them sewing the coarse material under a coal-oil lamp with fingers stiffening from the day's work. In too few hours they would have to walk back to Sister Henderson's Store, get vittles and load, again, onto the trucks. Then they would face another day of trying to earn enough for the whole year with the heavy knowledge that they were going to end the season as they started it. Without the money or credit necessary to sustain a family for three months. In cotton-picking time the late afternoons revealed the harshness of Black Southern life, which in the early morning had been softened by nature's blessing of grogginess, forgetfulness and the soft lamplight.

Revisit Your Strategy: Use Context Clues
Choose a word or phrase from the box that means the same as the **bold** word in each line from the autobiography. Write it on the line.

food	a store selling supplies	traveling musicians

1. "**troubadours** on their ceaseless crawlings through the South . . . sang their sad songs."

_____

2. "the staggering bill that waited on them at the white **commissary** downtown"

_____

3. "walk back to Sister Henderson's Store, get **vittles** and load, again, onto the trucks"

_____

Write any other unfamiliar word in this selection. Next, write the context clues that help explain its meaning. Finally, predict the meaning of the unfamiliar word and check your prediction in a dictionary.

_____

_____

After You Read

A. Comprehension Check

1. Angelou's grandmother, Mrs. Henderson, began her business in Stamps by
   (1) buying a store
   (2) selling lunches to area workers
   (3) starting a barbershop
   (4) opening a lunch counter

2. The Store became all of the following for the African Americans in Stamps *except*
   (1) a shop to buy whatever they needed
   (2) a place to meet, relax, and get a haircut
   (3) a boardinghouse for workers
   (4) a station where cotton pickers were picked up and returned

3. During cotton picking season, Mrs. Henderson began the day by
   (1) opening the store early
   (2) praying
   (3) washing the floor
   (4) ordering Maya to work in the fields

4. By picking cotton, people in Stamps were trying but failing to
   (1) pay off all their bills
   (2) supply the Store with cotton thread
   (3) earn their freedom
   (4) make extra money for luxuries

5. When Angelou says, "we became familiar enough to belong to the Store and it to us," we can infer that
   (1) the children grew to dislike the Store
   (2) they came to feel at home in the Store
   (3) the Store was always exciting to the children
   (4) the Store stopped meaning anything

6. The workers were always in debt because
   (1) they didn't work hard enough
   (2) they bought things they didn't need
   (3) they didn't know how to manage their money
   (4) their pay wasn't enough to live on

B. Read between the Lines

Check each statement that is likely to be true based on the reading selection.

_____ 1. Many people owed Mrs. Henderson money.
_____ 2. Mrs. Henderson had the only black-owned business in Stamps.
_____ 3. Picking cotton was very hard work that paid very little money.
_____ 4. The cotton pickers made a lasting impression on Maya.
_____ 5. Mrs. Henderson was unkind to Maya and her brother.
_____ 6. Mrs. Henderson was a hard-working woman.

C. Think beyond the Reading

Discuss these questions with a partner. Answer them in writing on separate paper if you wish.

1. How did the hard times that Maya saw as a child affect her as an adult? Do you think things we experience in childhood usually have lasting effects on us? Explain your answer.

2. Look back at your responses to the questions on page 46. Were the lives of the people in the story what you expected? Did you read anything that surprised you? If so, what?

Think About It: Analyze Setting

The selection you just read took place in a general store in a small Arkansas town. The events took place in the 1930s. Those facts—the place and the time—are the **setting** of the story. Details that Maya Angelou included help you imagine the setting. You also learned some of the feelings Angelou had for the store. The way an author describes a setting reflects how he or she feels about that place.

A. Look at Setting

In the paragraphs below, Angelou creates a picture of the setting that you can visualize. The three underlined phrases help you picture the setting as a store in a small town long ago.

1. Underline two more details in the first paragraph that help you picture *when* the story takes place.

> ▶ The formal name of the Store was the <u>Wm. Johnson General Merchandise Store</u>. Customers could find food staples, a good variety of colored thread, <u>mash for hogs</u>, <u>corn for chickens</u>, coal oil for lamps, light bulbs for the wealthy, shoe-strings, hair dressing, balloons, and flower seeds. Anything not visible had only to be ordered.
>
> Until we became familiar enough to belong to the Store and it to us, we were locked up in a Fun House of Things where the attendant had gone home for life.

You might have underlined "coal oil for lamps" and "light bulbs for the wealthy." They tell you the time was in the past when electric power in homes was rare and expensive.

2. Now underline a phrase in the second paragraph that helps you picture the store and reveals how Angelou felt about it.

The detail "a Fun House of Things" helps you picture a crowded setting full of items that are interesting, especially to children. It also helps you to know how Angelou felt about the store.

Tip An author can convey a setting by creating strong images with words. A good way for you to analyze a setting is to imagine what the place looks like as you read.

B. Practice

1. Reread the following excerpt from the selection. Then list the details that help you imagine the setting. One has been provided to help you get started. List at least three more.

   ▶ Each year I watched the field across from the Store turn caterpillar green, then gradually frosty white. I knew exactly how long it would be before the big wagons would pull into the front yard and load on the cotton pickers at daybreak to carry them to the remains of slavery's plantations.

   the field turning caterpillar green _____

   _____

   _____

   _____

2. Maya Angelou describes two settings: the Store in the morning and the Store in the late afternoon during cotton picking time. She compares the "tender mornings" with the late afternoon "harshness." She describes sounds and smells as well as sights to help you imagine each setting and understand the feelings it created. Reread the section that begins with "The lamplight in the Store" on pages 48–50. Complete the lists below with details that describe and create the feelings of these two different settings.

Tender Mornings	**Afternoon Harshness**
lamplight in the Store	_dying sunlight_
_____	_____
_____	_____
_____	_____

   ▶ **Talk About It**
   Interview one or two friends. Ask each person to name a favorite place. Then ask them to close their eyes for a moment, imagine the place, and tell you three or four important details (sights, sounds, smells) about it. Write each person's responses. Combine your results with those of your classmates. Draw conclusions about the kinds of places most people liked and the details they are most likely to remember.

Write About It: Describe a Setting

In the reading selection for this lesson, Maya Angelou described a setting from her childhood—her grandmother's store. Now you will have a chance to write about a setting that has meaning for you. First, study the sample.

Study the Sample

Read the steps below to see what the writer considered as he developed his description.

Step 1: Picking a Setting. The writer chose to describe a grade-school play he was in.

Step 2: Developing and Organizing Ideas. Here are the ideas the writer developed and listed for his description. Note that he included physical details and his feelings.

Place: elementary school cafeteria set up with a temporary stage
Time: the muggy night of my fourth-grade class play
Feelings: uncomfortable, nervous, tense, too warm
Details:

- blue curtain on poles and rods
- mothers in pastels and girdles
- fathers in blue suits and black shoes
- tables shoved off to side

- creaky wooden folding chairs
- waiting in "wings" behind curtains
- hushed and tense
- sweating into costume

Now read the writer's description on the next page. Then it will be your turn.

Your Turn

A. Prewriting

Step 1: The setting you choose should be one that you have strong feelings about. You may choose to write about some place from your childhood, or you may wish to write about a more recent setting. Here are some suggestions:

- childhood home
- grandparent's home
- a favorite place to play

- hospital
- church
- a private getaway spot

Choose your setting. In a few words, describe the feeling you wish to communicate.

Place: _____

Time: _____

Feelings: _____

One Nervous Night

Recently I was looking through a dusty box of family papers in my basement. I found an old photograph of myself taken nearly four decades ago on the night of my fourth-grade class play. One look at that skinny boy with the black-rimmed glasses standing in the worm costume, and the memory came rushing back.

It was a muggy May evening. The play took place in the school cafeteria, specially set up for the occasion. In front of and on each side of the temporary stage, a dusty, dark blue curtain hung on a makeshift array of poles and rods. The scarred metal lunch tables had all been pushed against the rear wall and into the corridor outside. On the scuffed-up cafeteria floor were rows of creaky wooden folding chairs. There our beaming parents and relatives sat.

At the time, they seemed like a frightening and impressive crowd. Dressed in a rainbow of pastel colors, mothers were stuffed into pinching girdles (women wore those back then). Fathers were all wearing shiny blue serge suits and shiny black dress shoes that usually came out of the closet once a week for an hour of church. They tugged at too-tight collars. I don't know who was more uncomfortable—the fourth-grade "actors" waiting in a hushed and tense sweat behind the curtain or the squirming members of the audience. By the time the play began, I was so nervous that I don't even remember walking on stage and reciting my lines!

Step 2: Visualize the setting you are going to write about. Close your eyes and concentrate. Think of details (sights, sounds, smells) that will make this setting real for your readers. On separate paper, list and organize the details you will include.

B. Writing

Describe the setting you have chosen. Think of a good title for your description.

Tip You can add new details that come to you as you are writing. Also notice that in the sample, the introduction explains what made the writer think about the long-ago memory and sets a context for the rest of the essay.

▶ **Save your draft.** At the end of this unit, you will work with one of your drafts further.

Lesson 5

LEARNING GOALS

Strategy: Use your background knowledge
Reading: Read a poem
Skill: Analyze tone
Writing: Write a personal response

Before You Read

In this lesson, you will read a poem expressing the thoughts and feelings of a man trying to find a job. Poetry concentrates a great deal of meaning into a few words and phrases. In a poem, each word is carefully selected and placed to convey emotion and create an effect. Every word in every line is important.

Before you begin reading, consider what you already know about poetry. Which of the following features do you expect to find in a poem?

_____ uneven line lengths	_____ a rhythm or beat
_____ rhyming words	_____ colorful images
_____ repeated words or phrases	_____ rules of capitalization not followed
_____ unnecessary words	_____ rules of punctuation not followed

Skilled readers use what they already know to understand what they read. Use what you know about the ways poetry can be written to help you understand the poem in this lesson.

Preview the Reading

Ask yourself what the title and the illustration suggest. Look at how the poem is printed on the page. Note how the poet uses short, broken lines to indicate how the speaker feels and to create an emotional effect in the reader. Notice the lack of punctuation marks and how capital letters are used.

Set Your Strategy: Use Your Background Knowledge

To help you understand this poem, you can use what you already know about poetry and what you know about being out of work. Have you ever been out of work for a long time? Or has someone you know spent a long time trying to find a job? If so, think about how it felt. What did you or that person do? Use your knowledge of that experience and of the elements of poetry as you read "A Job." After you read, you will analyze how your background knowledge helped you to understand the poem.

Bimbo Rivas is a young Puerto Rican poet. In this emotional poem, he describes the feelings of someone trying to find meaningful work.

A Job

Bimbo Rivas

A Job
to feed the time I spend adrift
in search for substance in the street
Awake at three a.m.
not knowing where or when the end   (5)
will come to my disdain
A Job
A simple job
A place to meet the day head on
with force and vigor   (10)
with fervor bigger than a winning independence slate
A Job
A Job my brain to put to work
My brain that tells me I'm OK
My brain that can produce the necessary rhythm   (15)
to set my idle body straight
My brain that yearns for a sincere break
I don't expect the world to stop for me
To stop its mission for my sake
I only ask for a clearer path   (20)
to put my brains and hands to work
to prove my worth
A Job

A Job my God
A Job that's better than the street   (25)
its hustle
and its pests
A Job
A Job that also fills my heart
not just my belly as does the city welfare   (30)
check
A Job with all the benefits
correlated with the sweat and time
invested by myself
A Job that don't step on my pride   (35)
A Job that don't shorten my life on earth
that will inspire me to help my bosses
their part of the proceeds collect
I need a JOB to keep my peace with God
A Job to make me stop wishing for an early grave   (40)
A Job
A Job
I NEED A JOB TODAY
Folks that got a job
a job that does its job   (45)
can see some sense in this relate
folks that lost their faith
that rot away with pain
DAY AFTER DAY
Strike at each other   (50)
hoping to find
in greater pain
a sedative
it's all too relative
my friends   (55)
A man without a JOB
is lost in the labyrinth[1] of
HELL.

---

1. **labyrinth** (LA/buh/rinth): a maze

▶ **Revisit Your Strategy: Use Your Background Knowledge**
Put a star (*) by all the lines in the poem you can understand especially well because of
your background knowledge.

After You Read

A. Comprehension Check

1. According to the speaker, what kind of job is he looking for?
   (1) a job where he uses his brain
   (2) an easy job
   (3) a job that pays extremely well
   (4) a factory job

2. A job will give the speaker all of the following *except*
   (1) a chance to prove his worth
   (2) a sense of meaning to his life
   (3) the right to scorn those who don't work
   (4) a place to meet the day head on

3. Getting a job will stop the speaker from what?
   (1) wishing he would die
   (2) trying to get a welfare check
   (3) taking drugs
   (4) begging on the street

4. According to the speaker, why do some people strike at one another?
   (1) to kill each other
   (2) to dull their own pain
   (3) to compete for work
   (4) to prove their worth

5. Which sentence best states the main idea of the poem?
   (1) A man needs a job to keep him off the streets.
   (2) A man needs a job that has benefits.
   (3) A man needs a job to challenge him and give him pride.
   (4) A man needs a break to get a job.

B. Read between the Lines

Check all the statements below that are probably true about the speaker in the poem.
Be ready to support your decisions.

_____ 1. When he has money to spend, he enjoys the excitement of the city streets.
_____ 2. He worries that others will think he is lazy.
_____ 3. He doesn't believe in God.
_____ 4. He has a low opinion of people who don't want to work.
_____ 5. He is too proud to take just any job that is offered.
_____ 6. He thinks of himself as a willing and hard worker.

C. Think beyond the Reading

Discuss these questions with a partner. Answer them in writing on separate paper if you wish.

1. The speaker explains the kind of job he wants: "A Job that don't step on my pride." Can a person be proud regardless of the kind of job he or she has? Explain.

2. Look back at the elements you checked on page 56. Did you find all the elements you expected in the poem? Did you find some things you didn't expect?

Think About It: Analyze Tone

When you read a poem like "A Job," you can sense the feelings behind the words. Those feelings are part of the poet's **tone.** Tone is an author's attitude toward the subject. The tone is an important part of an author's message.

The author's choice of words and details helps you sense the tone. For instance, if the poet had said, "A place to spend the day in useful occupation," rather than "A place to meet the day head on with force and vigor," the poem would lose energy and the tone would be less forceful.

The way the poet puts the words on the page also helps you identify the tone. Poets use line length to shape the poem. Poets may also use unusual capitalization, lack of punctuation, and other poetic elements.

A. Look at Tone

Reread the lines below from Bimbo Rivas's poem. Ask yourself what words, details, and poetic elements give you clues to the speaker's attitude toward his search for a job.

> ▶ I need a JOB to keep my peace with God
> A Job to make me stop wishing for an early grave
> A Job
> A Job
> I NEED A JOB TODAY

Check the words below that describe the tone of these lines.

____ desperate	____ encouraged	____ timid
____ tired	____ pleading	____ resigned

The repetition of the word *job,* the two short lines, and the capital letters help create a tone that is desperate and pleading.

Notice that the poet writes the word *job* three different ways in the poem. What are they?

_____   _____   _____

The word is written job, Job, and JOB. What effect does each form have on the tone? Read lines 39 through 46 aloud to sense the different emphasis of each form of the word. You can sense that capital letters create a loud, pleading tone. The more words are emphasized through the use of capital letters, the more loudly pleading the tone is.

Tip   When you read a poem, try to imagine the poet's tone of voice as if he or she were speaking the words aloud. If you hear the words in your mind, your experience will help you identify the tone.

B. Practice

Choose words from this box to answer questions 1, 2, and 3. You may use a word more than once.

angry	desperate	frantic	pleading
calm	fearful	humble	proud
demanding	forceful	irritated	reasonable

1. Read the first 22 lines of "A Job." Write three or four words that best describe the tone of this first part of the poem.

   _____

2. Read lines 23 through 40. Which words describe the tone of this part of the poem? Choose two or three.

   _____

3. Read from line 41 to the end of the poem. Which words from the list describe the tone at the end of the poem? Choose as many as you like.

   _____

4. How does the tone of the poem change from beginning to end?

   _____

   _____

▶ **Talk About It**

The poem you have just read expresses a man's thoughts and feelings about needing a job. Suppose the people listed below read the poem. Discuss the reaction each might have. Who might be critical or harsh? Who might be comforting or supportive? Who might offer advice? What kind of advice?

- the poet's mother
- the poet's father
- a friend of the poet
- a bill collector
- an employment counselor
- a job interviewer

Write About It: Write a Personal Response

In "A Job," Bimbo Rivas expressed his thoughts and feelings about being out of work and looking for a job. Now you will have a chance to write two personal responses to an event or situation in your life. You will practice using tone to express both a positive and a negative message. First, study the sample.

Study the Sample

The writer of the sample is a factory foreman. Read the steps below to see what he considered as he developed his two responses.

Step 1: Picking a Topic. The factory foreman chose giving feedback to a new worker as his topic.

Step 2: Developing and Organizing Ideas. The writer first listed the facts of the situation he chose. Then he thought of both positive and negative ways to interpret those facts. He used this chart to help him organize his ideas.

Facts	Positive Tone	Negative Tone
First day on the job	Don't be discouraged; beginning of successful learning	Carelessness; poor attention
Made mistakes	Made some errors	Damaged box of parts beyond repair; repeated mistakes
Must learn names and locations of parts	Difficult to do	Delivered some wrong parts
Must learn to operate forklift	Bill Owen will work with you; give you tips	Bill Owen will tell you what to do
Get one week of training	Will improve with practice; will be able to work on your own by end of week	If you get another poor performance rating at end of week, you will lose job.

Now read the writer's responses on the next page. Then it will be your turn.

Your Turn

A. Prewriting

Step 1: Think of an event or a situation in your own life about which you could write both a positive and a negative response. For instance, you might choose something that happened

- at work
- with a friend
- in your family
- in a relationship

Positive Response

Dear Art:

   Just a quick note to review your training yesterday. Although you made some errors, you shouldn't be discouraged. It is difficult to learn to operate a new piece of equipment and to learn the names and locations of dozens of unfamiliar machine parts. I think it was the beginning of a successful learning experience for you. And I'm sure that you will do better in this job as you get more practice. Remember that you have the whole rest of this week as a training period. I've assigned Bill Owen to work with you. He will watch you and give you tips. Pay attention to what Bill teaches you, and I'm sure that you will be able to do the job on your own by next week.

                                             Nelson

Negative Response

To: Trainee Arthur Hall

From: Nelson Giddes, Foreman

   Because of your carelessness and poor attention during your training yesterday, a box of parts was damaged beyond repair. You also made too many mistakes in delivering parts. Work on the assembly line was delayed. In the afternoon, you repeated the same time-wasting mistakes you made in the morning. I have assigned Bill Owen to observe and supervise you during the rest of this week. If your job performance has not improved by Friday, I will issue a second poor job performance rating, and your employment here will be terminated.

Step 2: List and organize your thoughts for two versions of your message—one with a positive tone and one with a negative tone. A chart like the one on page 62 will help.

B. Writing

Now write your two personal responses—one positive and one negative—on separate paper.

Tip
The way you address a response also reveals your tone. A note addressed "Dear Art" has a friendly, positive tone. A memo format has a formal, somewhat colder tone.

▶ **Save your draft.** At the end of this unit, you will work with one of your drafts further.

Lesson 6

LEARNING GOALS

Strategy: Visualize
Reading: Read an excerpt from a play
Skill: Analyze dialogue
Writing: Write a dialogue

Before You Read

The dialogue you are about to read is from Act 1 of *The Prisoner of Second Avenue,* a comedy by Neil Simon. The play is about a middle-aged business executive who may lose his well-paying job and the lifestyle that goes with it.

1. If you were such a person, how do you think you would feel?

_____

2. If you were married to a hardworking person who was suddenly afraid of losing his or her job, what would you say or do to try to make your spouse feel better?

_____

Neil Simon is one of Broadway's most successful playwrights. His plays are comedies, but they often contain serious elements. Think about and discuss how a play with a serious subject might still make people laugh.

Reading a play is different from reading a novel or short story. Plays do not include lengthy descriptions of the settings or the characters and their actions. There is usually a brief description of the setting and a list of characters, but most of what you read will be the dialogue, the lines the characters speak.

Preview the Reading

Look at the photographs. Notice that the characters are wearing bathrobes. Look at the script. Each speech is preceded by the name of the character who speaks it. Notice also the stage directions—in italics and set apart by parentheses. They tell the actors where to move and how to speak.

Set Your Strategy: Visualize

To get the most out of any reading, it is important to develop your visualizing skills. Visualizing means seeing in your own mind the images an author is creating with words. Because play scripts contain few descriptions, it is especially important to build mental images of what you think a scene looks like and how the characters act and feel. Try to picture in your mind what Mel and Edna look like, what they do, and how they act as you read this scene from *The Prisoner of Second Avenue.*

The Prisoner of Second Avenue *is set in Mel and Edna's apartment
in Manhattan. As the first scene opens, it is 2:30 in the morning in midsummer.
Mel has been unable to sleep and is very agitated. He has been yelling
at the neighbors and at Edna. Edna has unsuccessfully tried to calm him. She
has just angrily responded to Mel about his behavior, then turned to go to bed.*

The Prisoner of Second Avenue

Neil Simon

Anne Bancroft and Jack Lemmon in the 1974 movie version of *The Prisoner of Second Avenue*

MEL: Edna! *(She stops and turns around)* Don't go! . . . Talk to me for a few
minutes, because I think I'm going out of my mind.
(She stops, looks at him, and comes back into the living room)

EDNA: What is it?

MEL: I'm unraveling . . . I'm losing touch!

EDNA: You haven't been sleeping well lately.

MEL: I don't know where I am half the time. I walk down Madison Avenue, I think
I'm in a foreign country.

EDNA: I know that feeling, Mel.

MEL: It's not just a feeling, something is happening to me . . . I'm losing control. I
can't handle things any more. The telephone on my desk rings seven, eight
times before I answer it . . . I forgot how to work the water cooler today. I stood
there with an empty cup in my hand and water running all over my shoes.

EDNA: It's not just you, Mel, it's everybody. Everybody's feeling the tension these days.

MEL: Tension? If I could just feel tension, I'd give a thousand dollars to charity . . . When you're tense, you're tight, you're holding on to something. I don't know where to grab. Edna, I'm slipping, and I'm scared.

EDNA: Don't talk like that. What about seeing the analyst again?

MEL: Who? Doctor Pike? He's dead. Six years of my life, twenty-three thousand dollars. He got my money, what does he care if he gets a heart attack?

EDNA: There are other good doctors. You can see someone else.

MEL: And start all over from the beginning? "Hello. Sit down. What seems to be the trouble?". . . It'll cost me another twenty-three thousand just to fill *this* doctor in with information I already gave the dead one.

EDNA: What about a little therapy? Maybe you just need someone to talk to for a while.

MEL: I don't know where or who I am any more. I'm disappearing, Edna. I don't need analysts, I need Lost and Found.

EDNA: Listen . . . Listen . . . What about if we get away for a couple of weeks? A two-week vacation? Someplace in the sun, away from the city. You can get two weeks' sick leave, can't you, Mel?
(He is silent. He walks to the window and glances over at the plant)

MEL: Even the cactus is dying. Strongest plant in the world, only has to be watered twice a year. Can't make a go of it on Eighty-eighth and Second.

EDNA: Mel, answer me. What about getting away? Can't you ask them for two weeks off?

MEL: *(Makes himself a scotch)* Yes, I can ask them for two weeks off. What worries me is that they'll ask me to take the other fifty weeks as well.
(He drinks)

EDNA: You? What are you talking about? You've been there twenty-two years . . . Mel, is that it? Is that what's been bothering you? You're worried about losing your job?

MEL: I'm not worried about losing it. I'm worried about keeping it. Losing it is easy.

EDNA: Has something happened? Have they said anything?

MEL: They don't have to say anything. The company lost three million dollars this year. Suddenly they're looking to save pennies. The vice-president of my department has been using the same paper clip for three weeks now. A sixty-two-year-old man with a duplex on Park Avenue and a house in Southampton running around the office, screaming, "Where's my paper clip?"

EDNA: But they haven't actually said anything to you.

MEL: They closed the executive dining room. Nobody goes out to lunch any more. They bring sandwiches from home. Top executives, making eighty thousand dollars a year, eating egg-salad sandwiches over the wastepaper basket.

EDNA: Nothing has happened yet, Mel. There's no point in worrying about it now.

Jack Lemmon as Mel and Anne Bancroft as Edna

MEL: No one comes to work late any more. Everyone's afraid if you're not there on time, they'll sell your desk.

EDNA: And what if they did? We'd live, we'd get by. You'd get another job somewhere.

MEL: Where? I'm gonna be forty-seven years old in January. Forty-seven! They could get two twenty-three-and-a-half-year-old kids for half my money.

EDNA: All right, suppose something *did* happen? Suppose you *did* lose your job? It's not the end of the world. We don't have to live in the city. We could move somewhere in the country, or even out west.

MEL: And what do I do for a living? Become a middle-aged cowboy? Maybe they'll put me in charge of rounding up the elderly cattle . . . What's the matter with you?

EDNA: The girls are in college now, we have enough to see them through. We don't need much for the two of us.

MEL: You need a place to live, you need clothing, you need food. A can of polluted tuna fish is still eighty-five cents.

EDNA: We could move to Europe. To Spain. Two people could live for fifteen hundred dollars a year in Spain.

MEL: *(Nods) Spanish* people. I'm forty-seven years old, with arthritis in my shoulder and high blood pressure—you expect me to raise goats and live in a cave?

EDNA: You could work there, get some kind of job.

MEL: An advertising account executive? In Barcelona? They've probably been standing at the dock waiting for years for someone like that.

EDNA: *(Angrily)* What is it they have here that's so damned hard to give up? *What is it you'll miss so badly, for God's sakes?*

MEL: I'm not through with my life yet . . . I still have value, I still have worth.

EDNA: What kind of a life is this? You live like some kind of a caged animal in a Second Avenue zoo that's too hot in one room, too cold in another, over-charged for a growth on the side of the building they call a terrace that can't support a cactus plant, let alone two human beings. Is this what you call a worthwhile life? Banging on walls and jiggling toilets?

MEL: *(Shouts)* You think it's any better in Sunny Spain? Go swimming on the beach, it'll take you the rest of the summer to scrape the oil off.

EDNA: Forget Spain. There are other places to live.

MEL: Maine? Vermont maybe? You think it's all rolling hills and maple syrup? They have more people on welfare up there than they have pancakes. Washington? Oregon? Unemployed lumberjacks are sitting around sawing legs off chairs; they have nothing else to do.

EDNA: I will go anywhere in the world you want to go, Mel. I will live in a cave, a hut or a tree. I will live on a raft in the Amazon jungle if that's what you want to do.

MEL: All right, call a travel agency. Get two economy seats to Bolivia. We'll go to Abercrombie's tomorrow, get a couple of pith helmets and a spear gun.

EDNA: Don't talk to me like I'm insane.

MEL: I'm halfway there, you might as well catch up.

EDNA: I am trying to offer reasonable suggestions. I am not responsible. I am not the one who's doing this to you.

MEL: I didn't say you were, Edna.

EDNA: Then what do you want from me? *What do you want from anyone?*

MEL: *(buries his face in his hands)* Just a little breathing space . . . just for a little while.

▶ **Revisit Your Strategy: Visualize**

Reading a play is different from reading an autobiography or a story because it leaves so much to your imagination. List some of the things you visualized as you read the scene from *The Prisoner of Second Avenue*. Did Mel move a lot, or was he still? What was his tone of voice? How did Edna move and sound? What other details did you visualize?

_____

_____

_____

_____

_____

After You Read

A. Comprehension Check

1. Why is Mel afraid he is going to lose his job?
- (1) He is often late to work.
- (2) The company wants to hire younger people.
- (3) The company is losing money.
- (4) The company vice president thinks he wastes money.

2. How does Mel say he feels?
- (1) tense
- (3) feverish
- (2) not in control
- (4) eager for a change

3. Which of the following does Edna *not* suggest to help Mel?
- (1) start his own business
- (2) see a therapist
- (3) move away
- (4) go on vacation

4. In responding to Mel, Edna is generally
- (1) hysterical
- (3) uncaring
- (2) resentful
- (4) reassuring

5. By the way Mel talks about his six years of seeing an analyst, we can infer that
- (1) it helped him a lot
- (2) he had a good relationship with the analyst
- (3) he didn't get much out of it
- (4) he wished it hadn't ended

6. When Mel says, "I'm disappearing, Edna. I don't need analysts, I need Lost and Found," which word best describes his tone?
- (1) joking
- (3) confused
- (2) frantic
- (4) undecided

B. Read between the Lines

Check the statements on the left that you think are true of Mel. Check the ones on the right that you think are true of Edna. Look back at the play for evidence to support each statement you check.

Mel

____ **1.** He is afraid that someone will replace him at a lower salary.

____ **2.** He once felt content and competent.

____ **3.** He wants to keep Edna from worrying.

____ **4.** He no longer loves Edna.

____ **5.** He can't imagine having a different job or living anyplace else.

Edna

____ **1.** She is a worrier.

____ **2.** She complains and nags Mel.

____ **3.** She is loyal.

____ **4.** She loves Mel.

____ **5.** She is not happy with their Second Avenue apartment.

C. Think beyond the Reading

Discuss these questions with a partner. Answer them in writing on separate paper if you wish.

1. Who do you think is the "prisoner of Second Avenue" mentioned in the title? Why?

2. Think of your discussion about comedy and serious elements in Before You Read on page 64. How did this reading combine a serious subject and humor? Give at least two examples of dialogue you thought was funny, and explain why.

Think About It: Analyze Dialogue

A play script is mostly **dialogue**—conversation between the characters. When you read a novel or short story, the narrator describes the plot and the characters, even the characters' thoughts and feelings. When you read a play, these things must be communicated through the dialogue.

A. Look at Dialogue

Reread the excerpt of dialogue between Mel and Edna below. Think about what they say and also how they would say it. Notice all the information you can learn from this conversation—about the situation at Mel's office, about Mel and Edna as individuals, about them as a couple, and about how each of them feels about Mel's job situation.

> EDNA: You? What are you talking about? You've been there twenty-two years. . . Mel, is that it? Is that what's been bothering you? You're worried about losing your job?
>
> MEL: I'm not worried about losing it. I'm worried about keeping it. Losing it is easy.
>
> EDNA: Has something happened? Have they said anything?
>
> MEL: They don't have to say anything. The company lost three million dollars this year. Suddenly they're looking to save pennies. The vice-president of my department has been using the same paper clip for three weeks now. A sixty-two-year-old man with a duplex on Park Avenue and a house in Southampton running around the office, screaming, "Where's my paper clip?"
>
> EDNA: But they haven't actually said anything to you.
>
> MEL: They closed the executive dining room. Nobody goes out to lunch any more. They bring sandwiches from home. Top executives, making eighty thousand dollars a year, eating egg-salad sandwiches over the wastepaper basket.
>
> EDNA: Nothing has happened yet, Mel. There's no point in worrying about it now.
>
> MEL: No one comes to work late any more. Everyone's afraid if you're not there on time, they'll sell your desk.
>
> EDNA: And what if they did? We'd live, we'd get by. You'd get another job somewhere.

How do you think the actor playing Mel would sound saying his lines? Check any description you think would apply.

____ cheerful	____ fearful	____ resigned
____ emotional	____ furious	____ sarcastic

Mel is fearful that he is going to lose his job. His fear makes him emotional, and he uses a sarcastic tone to ridicule the people he works for.

Tip   Remember that plays are written to be spoken aloud. Try to hear the characters speaking their lines. Reading the dialogue aloud will help you understand it.

B. Practice

Answer these questions based on the excerpt of dialogue you just read.

1. **a.** Which details that Mel reports about the situation at his office are probably true?

   _____

   b. Which details that Mel reports are probably exaggerated for humor's sake?

   _____

2. Does Mel seem to be listening to Edna? How can you tell?

   _____

3. How do you think the actor playing Edna would sound saying her first four lines?
   Check any description that might apply.

   _____ cheerful   _____ disbelieving   _____ not really interested
   _____ concerned   _____ nervous   _____ relaxed

4. How do you think the actor playing Edna would sound saying her last line? Check
   any description that might apply.

   _____ comforting   _____ not really interested   _____ uncaring
   _____ concerned   _____ practical   _____ upset

5. Do you think Edna changes or stays the same in this scene? Explain.

   _____

▶ **Talk About It**
In this lesson, you read about the fears of a middle-aged executive who may lose his job. The play was written in 1971. Has the situation changed at all for people facing unemployment? List the fears people have now when they lose their job. Compare them with Mel's fears.

Write About It: Write a Dialogue

In this lesson, you read a dialogue between a husband and wife who are facing possible unemployment and a drastic change in their lives. Now you can write a dialogue between two people who are facing a hard decision or a problem. First, study the sample.

Study the Sample

Read the steps below to see what the writer considered as she developed her dialogue.

Step 1: Picking a Topic. The writer chose a situation in which a policeman is giving bad news to a mother about her children.

Step 2: Developing and Organizing Ideas. The writer answered the following questions to help her focus and decide what to write.

1. How will I start the dialogue?

    with the policeman introducing himself to the mother

2. How will I end it?

    with the mother's reaction to the news about her children's accident

3. Will each person contribute equally, or will one dominate?

    Both will contribute equally.

4. What do the characters sound like? What is each feeling?

    The policeman sounds formal, then kind.

    The woman sounds annoyed at first, then grows upset.

5. What stage directions will I need to include?

    how the scene starts; when the characters change their manner of speaking

Now read the writer's dialogue on the next page. Then it will be your turn.

Your Turn

A. Prewriting

Step 1: Think of two people who are facing a hard decision or problem. Choose an actual conversation you have heard, think of a conversation you would like to have, or invent a situation and conversation. Here are some suggestions.
- an engaged couple disagreeing about wedding plans
- a parent and child talking about something wrong the child did
- a disagreement with a neighbor
- two drivers involved in an accident

There is a knock on Esther's door. She goes to open it.

SERGEANT DIAS: Sergeant Alberto Dias, ma'am. May I inquire if you are Mrs. Esther Rollins?

ESTHER: *(a little annoyed)* Yes. What do you want? I'm in the middle of cooking. *(Looks more closely at Dias's face. Puts hand to her mouth.)* Is something wrong?

SERGEANT DIAS: Mrs. Rollins, a 1993 Oldsmobile registered to you was involved in a traffic accident today. Can you provide any information about who was operating the vehicle?

ESTHER: My son Danny took the car to pick up his sister at college. They're due home soon. *(She fully realizes something bad has happened.)* What's happened? Was Danny hurt? Was Antonia with him?

SERGEANT DIAS: *(in a kindly voice)* Perhaps you should take a seat, Mrs. Rollins. I need to ask you some questions.

ESTHER: *(worried and demanding)* Never mind about questions. I want answers right now! What's happened to my son. Is he hurt? Where is he? Where's my daughter?

SERGEANT DIAS: Mrs. Rollins, I'm afraid we don't know if your children are injured or even if they were in the car. About 45 minutes ago we received a report of an overturned car at the bottom of an embankment. The first officer on the scene reported that there was no one in or near the vehicle.

ESTHER: Danny! Toni! Oh no, what has happened! Where are my children? What can we do to find them?

Step 2: Ask and answer questions like those on page 72 to help you develop and organize your ideas.

B. Writing

On separate paper, write a dialogue between the two people you have chosen.

Tip See and hear the characters and their dialogue in your head. That will help you make them sound natural. It will also help you identify where you might need stage directions.

▶ **Save your draft.** At the end of this unit, you will work with one of your drafts further.

▶ Writing Skills Mini-Lesson: Complex Sentences

A complex sentence has two parts, an **independent clause** and a **dependent clause,** each with its own subject and verb:

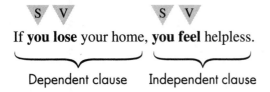

If **you lose** your home, **you feel** helpless.

Dependent clause   Independent clause

In the sentence above, the **dependent clause** begins with the connecting word *if.* Even though it has a subject and a verb, it does not make sense by itself. It cannot stand alone as a separate sentence. It depends on the independent clause to express a complete thought.

The second part of the example sentence is the **independent clause.** It is a complete thought, so it can stand alone. Here are some guidelines for writing complex sentences.

1. **Punctuation** You can put the dependent clause first or last in a sentence. If the dependent clause is first, put a **comma** after it. If the independent clause is first, do not use a comma.

    If you lose your home, you feel helpless.
    You feel helpless **if you lose your home.**

2. **Connecting words** A dependent clause begins with a dependent connecting word or phrase that indicates the relationship between the ideas in the two clauses. The chart below lists many of the common connecting words and phrases and the relationships they show. Notice that some words have more than one use.

Connecting Words and Phrases	Use to Show
after, as, as long as, as soon as, before, by the time, until, when, whenever, while	time relationships
as, because, in order that, since, so that	cause-and-effect relationships
if, in case, once, provided, unless	conditional relationships (conditions under which an event will occur)
although, even though, while	contrasting relationships

Practice

A. Fill in the blank in each sentence with the logical connecting word in parentheses. If a comma is necessary between the dependent and independent clause, add one. Then rewrite each sentence on the line provided. If the dependent clause came first, rewrite the sentence so that it comes at the end. If the independent clause came first, rewrite the sentence so that it comes at the end. Add commas where necessary. The first one is done as an example.

1 a. (When, Even though) _When_ we lost our home, we were desperate.

   b. _We were desperate when we lost our home._

2 a. (While, Because) _____ we had little money we had very few choices.

   b. _____

3 a. (if, unless) We'd be on the street _____ we could find a place to stay.

   b. _____

4 a. (since, until) We stayed at a shelter _____ we found an affordable apartment.

   b. _____

5 a. (Although, After) _____ the new apartment was old and small it was better than the shelter.

   b. _____

B. On separate paper, combine each pair of sentences to make a complex sentence. Use a logical connecting word, and add commas where necessary.

   1. My husband lost his job. We lost our home.
   2. There was room at the shelter. We weren't on the street.
   3. We were at the shelter. It was hard to sleep at night.
   4. There was noise and talking all night. The shelter was crowded.
   5. I like to cook. I missed being able to do my own cooking.
   6. I was grateful for the shelter. It was all we had.
   7. My husband found another job. We moved into a small apartment.
   8. I think about those weeks in the shelter. I'm grateful for our small apartment.

Unit 2 Review

Reading Review

Langston Hughes, an African American author, wrote novels, plays, and short stories, but is perhaps best known for his poetry. He often wrote of facing life's hard times with hope.

Mother to Son

Langston Hughes

Well, son, I'll tell you:
Life for me ain't been no crystal stair.
It's had tacks in it,
And splinters,
And boards torn up,
And places with no carpet on the floor—
Bare.
But all the time
I'se been a-climbin' on,
And reachin' landin's,

And turnin' corners,
And sometimes goin' in the dark
Where there ain't been no light.
So boy, don't you turn back.
Don't you set down on the steps
'Cause you finds it's kinder hard.
Don't you fall now—
For I'se still goin', honey,
I'se still climbin',
And life for me ain't been no crystal stair.

Choose the best answer to each question.

1. The mother speaking in the poem compares her life to
   (1) a glass house
   (2) a dark corner
   (3) a run-down stairway
   (4) a bare cupboard

2. What kind of life has the mother basically had?
   (1) successful   (3) tragic
   (2) rewarding   (4) hard

3. Which statement best sums up the main idea of the poem?
   (1) Just do the job you've been given and you'll stay out of trouble.
   (2) Don't give up; take what life gives you and move on.
   (3) You can't expect anyone to help you.
   (4) Never forget what I've sacrificed for you.

4. What is the mother's tone?
   (1) disappointed   (3) loving
   (2) defeated   (4) lecturing

Robert Fulghum, author of the bestseller All I Really Need to Know I Learned in Kindergarten *and other popular books, writes with humor about everyday life.*

A Modern Cinderella Story

Robert Fulghum

"Mister, you got a sense of humor?"

"Sure."

"I'll tell you most of a joke for a nickel."

"Most of a joke?"

"Right. And then for twenty cents I'll tell you the punch line."

"What if I don't want to know the punch line?"

"Hey—it's up to you. Take a chance, give me a nickel—what have you got to lose?"

Whenever I walk across this small city park, I get hit for a handout by those we commonly label "winos"—those burned-out, torn edges of the fabric of urban life who use this green square as an office, bedroom, social club, and toilet. As one explained to me, "We've gone to the dogs and even the dogs don't want us." The usual request is a muttered "Spare change?" or a more specific asking for a quarter for coffee. To cross the park is to cross an invisible toll bridge. I pay. And sometimes get a kind of fraternal blessing for my coin. "God bless you, brother."

It is not a joyful matter, this awkward asking and giving. And I know I could choose to walk around, instead of through, the park. Yet they are there, and I know it. I have spare change, and they know it. So we do what is to be done in the world-as-it-is-just-now. No matter what one does on behalf of the down-and-out and homeless, there is always this inescapable one-human-being-to-another engagement. This asking hand outstretched. At those times I cannot walk by and think or say that I gave money to some fund and voted for some laws and that I've done enough. I'd like to, but it just doesn't work that way.

Back to the park and the man offering part of a joke. I gave him a nickel, and he gave me a tale about a rabbi, a nun, a pig, and a chicken in a phone booth in Detroit. Outrageous joke. And he told it so well that I paid him five bucks for the punch line. It was a bargain. I laughed most of the rest of the afternoon as the story came back to mind. And I sent a few friends around to the park to check it out. I wasn't about to tell them the joke *or* the punch line for free.

The next day I learned that a small-scale vaudeville show was now part of the life of the park. A waitress in one of the nearby cafés, who daily went to smoke a cigarette there on her coffee breaks, befriended several of the winos. She actually talked to them.

She thought they were people. She convinced them to be more creative with their panhandling. They could be making twice as much for the same effort and have some fun as well. Why not? What did they have to lose?

This explains Mr. Part-of-a-Joke.

Other offerings from the cast include short poems, songs, advice, directions, excuses, card tricks, and quick fortunes. One guy offers to "laugh *with* you or *at* you for twenty-five cents." People now are attracted to the park who once avoided it. The new spirit may not last long, but for the time being, it is springtime there.

That waitress is a fairy godmother.

Not armed with a fancy magic wand, but with *compagination*—compassion mixed with imagination.

She touched the winos—not on their heads, but on their self-respect.

She did not give them pumpkins or shoes, but ideas about how they might come by these things.

She did not solve their problems but resolved the problem of food for one day.

She urged them to fish instead of begging for fishbones.

She offered them a glimpse of the truth that there are always options—which is called hope.

Choose the best answer to each question.

5. The dialogue at the beginning of the story is spoken between
   (1) a homeless person and the author
   (2) two "winos"
   (3) two comics
   (4) a waitress and a panhandler

6. Which of the following would you most likely find in the setting of this selection?
   (1) a toll bridge
   (2) a vaudeville stage
   (3) a restaurant
   (4) a bench

7. According to the author, the waitress helped the panhandlers in the park most when she
   (1) gave them money
   (2) laughed at their jokes
   (3) treated them with respect
   (4) gave them cigarettes

8. What is the author's tone when he writes about the "winos"?
   (1) disgusted
   (2) compassionate
   (3) critical
   (4) excited

The Writing Process

In Unit 2, you wrote three first drafts. Choose below the draft that you would like to work with further. You will revise, edit, and make a final copy of this draft.

_____ your description of a setting on pages 54–55

_____ your personal responses to an event or situation on pages 62–63

_____ your dialogue between two people on pages 72–73

Find the first draft you chose. Then turn to page 176 in this book. Follow steps 3, 4, and 5 in the Writing Process to create a final draft.

As you revise, check your draft for these specific points.

Description of a setting: Have you included details that make the setting real—that help readers visualize the setting and get a feel for it?

Personal response: Does your choice of words reflect the positive or negative tone you are trying to create in each response?

Dialogue: Have you written the two speakers' parts so that they sound natural? Have you inserted stage directions where they are needed?

Unit 3 Then and Now

One of the few things in life we can be sure about is that time will pass—and things will change. Sometimes we may long for the "good old days." But we also know the truth of the saying "That was then; this is now." In this unit, you will read the words of people who have lived both then and now—people who are more than 100 years old. You will discover what a woman learned from her mother and grandmother, and what she in turn taught her own daughter. And you will learn what life was like for a group of workers on an assembly line in the 1950s.

Before you begin Unit 3, think about your own past and the past of your parents and grandparents. How were those times like the present? How were they different? If you could return to some moment in your own past, what moment would you choose? Why?

▶ **Be an Active Reader**

As you read the selections in this unit
- Put a question mark (?) by things you do not understand.
- Underline words you do not know. Try to use context clues to figure them out.

After you read each selection in this unit
- Reread sections you marked with a question mark. If they still do not make sense, discuss them with a partner or your instructor.
- Look at words you underlined. Discuss any words you still don't know the meaning of with a partner or your instructor, or look them up in a dictionary.

Lesson 7

LEARNING GOALS

Strategy: Use your background knowledge
Reading: Read an informative article
Skill: Compare and contrast
Writing: Write a comparison and contrast essay

Before You Read

The article in this lesson is about the memories and experiences of some people who are more than 100 years old.

1. What do you think it feels like physically and emotionally to have lived for more than 100 years?

   _____

2. Think about the events and changes that a person who has lived for 100 years has seen. Look at the list below. Check all that you think are among the most important social and political events of the 1900s. Add other events or changes if you like.

   _____ World War I   _____ civil rights movement   _____ space exploration
   _____ Great Depression   _____ women's movement   _____ movies and TV
   _____ World War II   _____ sexual revolution   _____ computers

   _____   _____   _____

3. If you were transported 100 years back in time, what would be hard for you to adjust to? What would you miss most about the present?

   _____

Preview the Reading

Read the introduction and the title, and look at the pictures. Then read the first and last paragraphs to get an idea of what you will be reading about.

Set Your Strategy: Use Your Background Knowledge

You probably know more than you think you do about the last 100 years. Your parents, grandparents, perhaps even your great-grandparents lived during this period. What do you know about their lives? On separate paper, make a two-column chart with the headings *What I Already Know* and *What I Learned.* In the first column, write several things that you know about the last 100 years. The topics listed in question 2 above can help you. Use what you know about these topics to help you understand the article as you read. You will have a chance to fill in the other column when you finish reading.

There are 12 times more people over 100 living today than in the 1960s. What have these people seen and learned in their lives? How do they feel about having lived so long? The author of this article reflects on their experiences.

Our Century

Lynn Rosellini

New York City street scene around 1910.

They sit, gnarled[1] hands gripping the sides of their wheelchairs or toying with the handles of canes. When they speak, the words come unhurriedly, in voices that crack and sometimes trail into silence. But if the day is a good one, if they have slept well and the physical indignities of age do not impinge,[2] then the decades gradually begin to fall away. A tear curls down a withered[3] cheek. A hoot of laughter erupts. Images—immediate and tangible[4] and visceral[5]—slowly materialize. And for a brief moment, you can read all of America's past century in their eyes.

For a moment it is 1908, and 15-year-old Ora Glass gazes overhead at an airplane in Omaha. "I thought the world was coming to an end," she murmurs, her faded eyes widening again at the memory. For a moment it is

---

1. gnarled (narld): twisted, knotted, deformed
2. impinge (im/PINJ): intrude, break in on
3. withered: shriveled, wrinkled
4. tangible (TAN/juh/bul): able to be touched or felt
5. visceral (VI/seh/rul): internal, emotional

1920, and Italian immigrant Dominic Cali, then 27, stands on a ship with his heart racing at the sight of the Statue of Liberty: "Those big open arms of hers said, 'C'mon, boy. Come to me.'"

Women campaigning for the right to vote in the early 20th century.

Glass and Cali are two of 52,000 centenarians[6] in America today, more than 12 times the number just 30 years ago. Together, they form a precious national treasure, a collective conscience of sorts for the century in which the American dream of prosperity by and large came true. They witnessed a transformation unmatched in history: From horse-drawn wagons to the space shuttle, from washboards to Whirlpools, from quill pens to computer keyboards. They saw two world wars, communism's rise and fall, the civil rights revolution and the women's movement. During their lives, America more than tripled in population and shifted from isolation to the only super-power in the world, from a young nation with an average life expectancy of 47 years to a graying one, with a norm[7] of 75.5 years.

For a few centenarians, like the Delany sisters, whose autobiography [*Having Our Say,* published in 1993] illuminating racial discrimination be-came a bestseller and spawned[8] a Broadway play, age has brought celebrity. For most, their well-worn tales are saved for great-grandchildren or an occasional newspaper reporter. But the story they relate is worth cherishing for its perspective on an era that is often misunderstood.

The 20th century is one that fits the vision of neither conservatives nor liberals, though both try to define the past in ways that support their versions

6. centenarians (sen/tuh/NEHR/ee/uns): persons 100 years old or older
7. norm: average
8. spawned: produced, gave birth to

of the present. Conservatives look at the past 100 years and bemoan what the nation has lost: strong families, hard work, close ties to the church and safe streets. Liberals look at the same era and celebrate progress: the end of *de jure*[9] discrimination and sweeping reductions in illiteracy, poverty, ill health and sexism. Yet the people who have *lived* for 100 years say that it was better *and* worse.

Real change. Consider the role of rules. America in 1895 was a society bound by morés[10] regulating everything from the length of women's dresses (covering the ankles) to social conversation (sex, spouse abuse, homosexuality and mental illness were all taboo[11]). Children addressed their elders as "Sir" and "Ma'am" (back talk warranted the strap). Such rules offered people a reassurance of their place in the universe.

But there was a downside. Many homes were filled with loveless marriages and repressed emotions. Women couldn't vote and couldn't teach school if they were married. Listen to 100-year-old Mary Okinaga: "I didn't like him," she says of her husband of 40-odd years, who had been picked by her father. Why? "He used to beat me, especially after drinking." Did she think about leaving? "Divorce was not an option."

It's tempting to romanticize the material hardships of the past. The image recalled by 101-year-old Annie Healey of her father sitting at night in Massachusetts with tacks in his mouth, tapping soles for his kids' shoes because they couldn't afford new ones, is worthy of Norman Rockwell.

Yet except for the wealthy, daily life usually entailed crushing labor. In 1900, 70 percent to 80 percent of Americans lived in poverty, and half did so by the end of the 1920s. Men farmed with horses, mules and the strength of their own backs. Women's brutal job was housekeeping: A simple task like laundry took half a day—from boiling the water to pulling wash off the clothesline (frozen stiff, in winter). True, some may have read books. But 1 out of 10 people couldn't read a simple message.

Perhaps the most pervasive[12] bit of Americana, though, is the notion that people were friendlier in the first decades of this century. They knew their neighbors, helped each other without being asked and chatted on front porches in the evenings. Cali recalls it "was all friendly." Unless, of course, you were non-white or non-Christian. It is easy to forget that many white Americans hated and feared blacks at the turn of the century, and even as recently as 1945, a majority of whites supported segregation. Centenarian Joseph Goldstein recalls the taunts of his Boston childhood: "Kill the Jews." And May Childs, a 104-year-old Crow Indian woman, can still conjure[13] up the "No Indians Wanted" signs in Billings, Mont.

---

9. *de jure* (dee/JOOR/ee): legal Latin term for "by law"
10. morés (MORE/ayz): traditional customs and behaviors
11. taboo: a forbidden act, object, or topic
12. pervasive (per/VAY/siv): spread throughout
13. conjure (KON/joor): to summon up or recall

Four major 20th-century events (clockwise from right-hand side): *Apollo 11* takes off for the moon; troops raise the U.S. flag on Iwo Jima; President Franklin Roosevelt addresses the nation on radio; men wait in a Depression-era bread line.

Still, centenarians agree that there was something wondrous about the early part of the century, a sense that one could make of life anything one chose. These 100-year-olds appear to have retained that same positive outlook. "I still am learning, every day," says Pauline McCleve, 100, of Tempe, Ariz. Nor do they hang on to hardships and grief. "I don't occupy my mind with things that are not necessary," says Sidney Amber, 109, of San Francisco.

These days, they have far less to worry them. Fingers that once scrubbed laundry on washboards now toy with knitting. Hands that once controlled lumbering plow horses now maneuver bingo chips. And lips that sang lullabies in candle-lit nurseries now move to tell their bygone tales.

▶ **Revisit Your Strategy: Use Your Background Knowledge**
Go back to the chart you started for Set Your Strategy on page 80. Put a check mark in front of each fact or event you listed that was also mentioned in the article. In the second column, write some of the things you learned about the last 100 years from reading this article.

After You Read

A. Comprehension Check

1. The average life expectancy in 1900 was
   - (1) 47 years
   - (3) 75 years
   - (2) 57.5 years
   - (4) 100 years

2. The past 100 years have seen an increase in
   - (1) physical labor
   - (3) legal discrimination
   - (2) U.S. global power
   - (4) sexism

3. One difference between U.S. society 100 years ago and today is that people then
   - (1) divorced more frequently
   - (2) had a more negative outlook
   - (3) were healthier
   - (4) followed stricter social rules

4. Compared with 100 years ago, the number of people living in poverty today is
   - (1) slightly larger
   - (3) half as much
   - (2) about the same
   - (4) much lower

5. From the sentence "Children addressed their elders as 'Sir' and 'Ma'am' (back talk warranted the strap)," you can infer that
   - (1) children were always polite to older people
   - (2) older people treated children with respect
   - (3) physical punishment of children was acceptable
   - (4) children were seldom punished for showing disrespect

6. Which sentence best states the main idea of the article?
   - (1) America's centenarians can remember seeing airplanes for the first time.
   - (2) America's centenarians hold precious memories of the vast changes of the 20th century.
   - (3) America's centenarians can remember what it was like when society had more rules.
   - (4) America's centenarians remember how hard life was in the early 1900s.

B. Read between the Lines

Check each statement below that you might infer from information in the article. Look back at the article for evidence to support your choices.

_____ 1. People tend to look back at history and read what they want into events.

_____ 2. Nine out of 10 people read books 100 years ago.

_____ 3. Housework left many women with little time to do anything else 100 years ago.

_____ 4. Most people over 100 years old actually have few physical problems.

_____ 5. The idea that people were friendlier earlier in this century is only partly correct.

_____ 6. Love and happiness have always been the most important reasons for marriage.

C. Think beyond the Reading

Think about the reading, and discuss it with a partner. Answer the questions in writing on separate paper if you wish.

1. If you live to be 100, do you think the changes you see will be as great as today's centenarians have seen in their lives? What will change the most? The least?

2. Look back at your response to question 3 in Before You Read on page 80. Did anything in the article make you want to change your answer at all? If so, what?

Think About It: Compare and Contrast

The article "Our Century" describes some of the great changes that have taken place in the U.S. over the last 100 years. The author compared and contrasted the present and the past to illustrate some of these changes. When you **compare,** you look for things that are alike; to **contrast,** you look for things that are different.

A. Look at Comparison and Contrast

The following excerpt from "Our Century" shows how the author compares and contrasts life in the early 1900s with life in the 1990s.

> ▶ They witnessed a transformation unmatched in history: From horse-drawn wagons to the space shuttle, from washboards to Whirlpools, from quill pens to computer keyboards.

The passage compares and contrasts items in three categories. This chart lists the three categories. Complete the chart with information from the passage.

Early 1900s	Category	Now
horse-drawn wagons	travel	space shuttle
washboards	laundry methods	_____
_____	writing tools	_____

The past and the present are alike in that people traveled, did laundry, and wrote during both. But the horse-drawn wagons of the past and the space shuttle of the present are vastly different. So are washboards and Whirlpool washing machines, as well as quill pens and computer keyboards.

 Tip
In this passage the repeated word pattern *from . . . to . . .* indicates contrasts between the two time periods. Other clue words that indicate **contrast** include *but, however, still, on the other hand, instead of, conversely, although, unlike,* and *nevertheless.* Clue words that indicate **comparisons** are *like, likewise, as . . . as, both . . . and, in the same way,* and *similarly.*

B. Practice

1. Use information in this excerpt to complete the next chart.

> ▶ America more than tripled in population and shifted from isolation to the only superpower in the world, from a young nation with an average life expectancy of 47 years to a graying one, with a norm of 75.5 years.

Then	Point of Contrast	Now
_____	foreign policy and status	_____
_____	life expectancy	_____

2. In the section titled "Real change" on page 83, the author mentions social rules of 1895 that have changed. List three of these rules in the first column below. In the second column, describe in your own words the contrasting behavior that is accepted today.

Society's Rules in the 1890s	Society's Rules in the 1990s
_____	_____
_____	_____
_____	_____

3. In the same section on page 83, the author discusses four areas of major change listed below. In the first column, give an example of what life was like before each change. In the second column, give a contrasting example of what life is like now.

Before	Point of Contrast	After
_____	women's suffrage	_____
_____	farm work	_____
_____	housekeeping	_____
_____	civil rights movement	_____

▶ **Talk About It**

Interview the oldest person you know about the changes he or she has seen. Beforehand, list questions to ask; take brief notes on the answers. Share your findings with your classmates.

Write About It: Write a Comparison and Contrast Essay

The author of "Our Century" compared and contrasted life in the U.S. 100 years ago with life today. In this section you will have a chance to write an essay comparing and contrasting situations, places, or people in your own life. First, study the sample.

Study the Sample

Read the steps and the chart below to see what the writer considered as he developed his comparison and contrast essay.

Step 1: Picking a Topic. The writer of the example below chose to compare and contrast himself with his father.

Step 2: Developing and Organizing Your Ideas. This chart shows how the writer developed his ideas for his comparison and contrast essay.

Me	Characteristic	My Father
35	Age	when he was 35
6 feet, thin, balding, beard, glasses	Appearance	6 feet, thinner, balding, beard, glasses
divorced twice, 1 child	Marital status	married 10 years, 3 children
always searching for something more	Personality	relaxed, content
real estate salesman	Work	owned fruit orchard
sports coats, designer labels	Clothing	jeans, work shirts
music	Recreation	outdoors, fishing

Now read the writer's comparison and contrast essay on the next page. Then it will be your turn.

Your Turn

A. Prewriting

Step 1: Choose one of the topics below to compare and contrast, or choose another topic.

- a parent or grandparent and you
- your current home and the home you grew up in
- your community 10 or 20 years ago and the way it is now
- your first car and the car you have now

My Father and Me

When I look at pictures of my father in old family photo albums, I sometimes think I'm seeing a mirror image of myself. The 35-year-old man in the pictures and the 35-year-old me look astonishingly alike. We are both about six feet tall and on the thin side. Our hair—what's left of it—is nearly the same color. We both wear glasses, and we both have beards of dark and blond hair mixed with gray. But the similarities end there.

My father has always been devoted to his marriage and three kids. All his working life has been spent tending the orchard he and my mother own. My father loves the outdoors. When he isn't busy planting, pruning, or picking, my father loves to go fishing. As you might expect, he is most comfortable in worn jeans and work shirts and wears them all the time. All in all, my father is a very contented man.

On the other hand, I am restless and always searching for something more. I have been divorced twice and have a daughter I see only on weekends. Unable to find a satisfying career, I've moved from job to job. For the past two years, I've been with a real estate firm, though I may not stay there much longer. I wear suits or sports coats when I'm working, but I prefer designer casuals when I'm not. In my free time, I like to go out and listen to live music. I have loved rock music all my life, and my father—not surprisingly—has always hated it.

Step 2: List your ideas. Then decide how you will organize your ideas. Will you write about all the points of comparison first, and then the points of contrast? Or will you write about first one subject and then the other? Or will you use a combination of styles?

B. Writing

On separate paper, write your comparison and contrast essay.

Tip To help readers follow your comparison and contrast, use clue words like those listed on page 86. To help you organize your ideas, fill in a comparison and contrast chart.

▶ **Save your draft.** At the end of this unit, you will work with one of your drafts further.

Lesson 8

LEARNING GOALS

Strategy: Empathize
Reading: Read a personal essay
Skill: Make inferences
Writing: Write a personal essay

Before You Read

In the essay that follows, Patricia Raybon writes about her attitude toward housekeeping tasks—especially washing windows—in her old, slightly run-down house. Before you read the essay, think about the following questions and write responses.

1. List some of the housekeeping chores you do.

_____

2. How did you learn to do these things?

_____

3. What is your attitude toward housekeeping chores? Are there things you like to do? What enjoyment do you get from doing them? Are there things you hate or refuse to do? What are they? Why do you dislike them?

_____

_____

_____

Preview the Reading

Read the introduction, the title, and the first two paragraphs. Then think for a moment about the title and what it refers to. Look at the illustrations to learn more of what the essay may be about.

Set Your Strategy: Empathize

When you empathize, you identify with someone else's thoughts and feelings. Empathy leads you to a deeper understanding of the people you are reading about. As you read this essay, try to empathize with the author. Try to feel what she feels toward her mother and grandmother and the lessons they taught her. When you finish reading, you will have a chance to identify some of her thoughts and feelings.

In this personal essay, the author writes of the pleasure and pride she finds in simple household tasks—one task in particular—and how such feelings have been passed from generation to generation.

Letting In Light

Patricia Raybon

The windows were a gift or maybe a bribe—or maybe a bonus—for falling in love with such a dotty old house. The place was a wreck. A showoff, too. So it tried real hard to be more. But it lacked so much—good heat, stable floors, solid walls, enough space. A low interest rate.

But it had windows. More glass and bays and bows than people on a budget had a right to expect. And in unlikely places—like the window inside a bedroom closet, its only view a strawberry patch planted by the children next door.

None of it made sense. So we bought the place. We saved up and put some money down, then toasted the original builder—no doubt some brave and gentle carpenter, blessed with a flair for the grand gesture. A romantic with a T-square.[1]

We were young then and struggling. Also, we are black. We looked with irony and awe at the task now before us. But we did not faint.

The time had come to wash windows.

Yes, I do windows. Like an amateur and a dabbler, perhaps, but the old-fashioned way—one pane at a time. It is the best way to pay back something so plain for its clear and silent gifts—the light of day, the glow of moon, hard rain, soft snow, dawn's early light.

The Romans called them *specularia*. They glazed their windows with translucent marble and shells. And thus the ancients let some light into their world.

In my own family, my maternal grandmother washed windows—and floors and laundry and dishes and a lot of other things that needed cleaning—while doing day work for a rich, stylish redhead in her Southern hometown.

To feed her five children and keep them clothed and happy, to help them walk proudly and go to church and sing hymns and have some change in their pockets—and to warm and furnish the house her dead husband had built and added onto with his own hands—my grandmother went to work.

She and her third daughter, my mother, put on maids' uniforms and cooked and sewed and served a family that employed my grandmother until she was nearly 80. She called them Mister and Missus—yes, ma'am and yes, sir—although she was by many years their elder. They called her Laura. Her surname[2] never crossed their lips.

But her daughter, my mother, took her earnings from the cooking and serving and window washing and clothes ironing and went to college, forging a life with a young husband—my father—that granted me, their daughter, a lifetime of relative comfort.

I owe these women everything.

They taught me hope and kindness and how to say thank you.

They taught me how to brew tea and pour it. They taught me how to iron creases and whiten linen and cut hair ribbon on the bias so it doesn't unravel. They taught me to carve fowl, make butter molds and cook a good cream sauce. They taught me "women's work"—secrets of home, they said, that now are looked on mostly with disdain[3]: how to sweep, dust, polish and wax. How to mow, prune, scrub, scour and purify.

They taught me how to wash windows.

Not many women do anymore, of course. There's no time. Life has us all

---

1. T-square: a measuring tool shaped like a capital T used by carpenters to create square corners and draw parallel lines

2. surname: the last or family name of a person

3. disdain (dis/DAYN) scorn; contempt

on the run. It's easier to call a "window man," quicker to pay and, in the bargain, forget about the secret that my mother and her mother learned many years before they finally taught me.

Washing windows clears the cobwebs from the corners. It's plain people's therapy, good for troubles and muddles and other consternations.[4] It's real work. I venture—honest work—and it's a sound thing to pass on. Mother to daughter. Daughter to child. Woman to woman.

This is heresy,[5] of course. Teaching a girl to wash windows is now an act of bravery—or else defiance. If she's black, it's an act of denial, a gesture that dares history and heritage to make something of it.

But when my youngest was 5 or 6, I tempted fate and ancestry and I handed her a wooden bucket. Together we would wash the outdoor panes. The moment sits in my mind:

She works a low row. I work the top. Silently we toil, soaping and polishing, each at her own pace—the only sounds the squeak of glass, some noisy birds, our own breathing.

Then, quietly at first, this little girl begins to hum. It's a nonsense melody, created for the moment. Soft at first, soon it gets louder. And louder. Then a recognizable tune emerges. Then she is really singing. With every swish of the towel, she croons louder and higher in her little-girl voice with her little-girl song. "This little light of mine—I'm gonna let it shine! Oh, this little light of mine—I'm gonna let it shine!" So, of course, I join in. And the two of us serenade the glass and the sparrows and mostly each other. And too soon our work is done.

"That was fun," she says. She is innocent, of course, and does this work by choice, not by necessity. But she's not too young to look at truth and

4. **consternations** (kon/stir/NAY/shunz) extreme worries; dismay
5. **heresy** (HEHR/uh/see): an opinion or belief that disagrees with what is commonly accepted

understand it. And her heart, if not her arm, is resolute and strong.

Those years have passed. And other houses and newer windows—and other "women's jobs"—have moved through my life. I have chopped and puréed and polished and glazed. Bleached and folded and stirred. I have sung lullabies.

I have also marched and fought and prayed and taught and testified. Women's work covers many bases.

But the tradition of one simple chore remains. I do it without apology.

Last week, I dipped the sponge into the pail and began the gentle bath—easing off the trace of wintry snows, of dust storms and dead, brown leaves, of too much sticky tape used to steady paper pumpkins and Christmas lights and crepe-paper bows from holidays now past. While I worked, the little girl—now 12—found her way to the bucket, proving that her will and her voice are still up to the task, but mostly, I believe, to have some fun.

We are out of step, the two of us. She may not even know it. But we can carry a tune. The work is never done. The song is two-part harmony.

▶ **Revisit Your Strategy: Empathize**

1. Think about the situation described in the excerpt below. Check one or more words below that describe what you think the author was feeling at the time.

> ▶ None of it made sense. So we bought the place. We saved up and put some money down, then toasted the original builder—no doubt some brave and gentle carpenter, blessed with a flair for the grand gesture. A romantic with a T-square.
>
> We were young then and struggling. Also, we are black. We looked with irony and awe at the task now before us. But we did not faint.

How did the author feel when they decided to buy the house?

_____ challenged   _____ distressed   _____ foolish   _____ determined   _____ excited

2. Think about the situation described in the excerpt below. Choose one or more words from each row that describe what you think the daughter and mother were feeling at the time.

> ▶ Silently we toil, soaping and polishing, each at her own pace. . . . Then, quietly at first, this little girl begins to hum. It's a nonsense melody, created for the moment. Soft at first, soon it gets louder. And louder. Then a recognizable tune emerges. Then she is really singing.

a. How did the little girl feel as she washed windows?

_____ engrossed   _____ sore   _____ joyful   _____ silly   _____ tired

b. How did the author feel as she heard her little girl?

_____ bored   _____ irritated   _____ pleased   _____ glad   _____ proud

After You Read

A. Comprehension Check

1. One reason the author fell in love with her old house was its
   (1) strawberry patch next door
   (2) solid walls and plenty of space
   (3) many windows
   (4) low interest rate

2. The author enjoys washing windows because it gives her all the following *except*
   (1) time to think
   (2) light coming into her home
   (3) extra money
   (4) pride in work

3. The author knew her 6-year-old daughter enjoyed washing windows when the daughter
   (1) told her mother so
   (2) asked to learn how to wash windows
   (3) began to wash windows without being asked
   (4) hummed and sang as she washed windows

4. Which word best describes the author's tone when she says, "It is the best way to pay back something so plain for its clear and silent gifts"?
   (1) confused   (3) disinterested
   (2) grateful   (4) sarcastic

5. Unlike her mother's and grandmother's, the author's "women's work" included
   (1) marching and testifying
   (2) cleaning and cooking
   (3) washing windows
   (4) doing laundry

6. In the sentence "They glazed their windows with *translucent* marble and shells," *translucent* means
   (1) unbreakable   (3) polished
   (2) very thin   (4) almost transparent

B. Read between the Lines

Check each statement that you think the author would agree with. Look back at the essay for evidence to support your choices.

_____ 1. Teaching a girl housework is unpopular because people think it is too traditional.

_____ 2. Sometimes being out of step with the times is all right.

_____ 3. Men should not have to do housework.

_____ 4. It is embarrassing to have a mother who worked as a maid.

_____ 5. It is pleasing to have a daughter who likes washing windows.

_____ 6. Buying the "dotty old house" was a mistake.

_____ 7. It is satisfying to apply the skills learned from your mother.

C. Think beyond the Reading

Think about this essay, and discuss it with a partner. Answer the questions in writing on separate paper if you wish.

1. How does the author's attitude affect the way she washes windows? How can attitude help when you are doing something you may not want to do?

2. Read what you wrote about your attitude toward housework on page 90. How did it compare with the author's? Has reading the essay changed your attitude at all?

Think About It: Make Inferences

When you answered the questions in Read between the Lines on page 95, you were making **inferences.** To make inferences, you combine clues from the reading selection with your own knowledge and experience to figure out things that the author did not actually state.

A. Look at Making Inferences

Reread the following excerpt from the essay. Look for clues about the author and her husband and about the house.

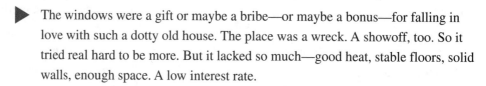

> The windows were a gift or maybe a bribe—or maybe a bonus—for falling in love with such a dotty old house. The place was a wreck. A showoff, too. So it tried real hard to be more. But it lacked so much—good heat, stable floors, solid walls, enough space. A low interest rate.
>
> But it had windows. More glass and bays and bows than people on a budget had a right to expect. And in unlikely places—like the window inside a bedroom closet, its only view a strawberry patch planted by the children next door.

Can you infer that the author and her husband at times make decisions based on emotion rather than logic? Yes, because the house was "dotty" and a "wreck," but they fell "in love" with it and bought it anyway. Can you infer that the house was over-priced? No, because you know only that it lacked a low interest rate. The asking price of the house still could have been fair.

Now check each statement below that you can infer.

_____ The house attracted attention in the neighborhood.

_____ The author and her husband did not care about the cost of the house.

If you checked the first statement, you are correct. The author calls the house a "showoff," implying that it called attention to itself. However, you cannot infer the second statement. In fact, you can infer that the cost did concern them because she comments on the interest rate, and she says they were "people on a budget."

 Tip Make sure you have enough evidence to make an inference. Don't read too much between the lines.

B. Practice

Read the following excerpt and the statements below it. Write *Yes* next to each statement that can be inferred from the excerpt. Write *No* if the statement cannot be inferred. Then explain your answer.

► In my own family, my maternal grandmother washed windows—and floors and laundry and dishes and a lot of other things that needed cleaning—while doing day work for a rich, stylish redhead in her Southern hometown.

To feed her five children and keep them clothed and happy, to help them walk proudly and go to church and sing hymns and have some change in their pockets —and to warm and furnish the house her dead husband had built and added onto with his own hands—my grandmother went to work.

She and her third daughter, my mother, put on maids' uniforms and cooked and sewed and served a family that employed my grandmother until she was nearly 80. She called them Mister and Missus—yes, ma'am and yes, sir—although she was by many years their elder. They called her Laura. Her surname never crossed their lips.

Can you infer that

_____ **1.** the grandmother was not rich and stylish?

_____

_____ **2.** the grandmother got no help with the housework in her own home?

_____

_____ **3.** the grandmother became a widow early in life?

_____

_____ **4.** the author is proud of her grandmother's accomplishments?

_____

_____ **5.** the author's mother was forced by the grandmother to work as a maid?

_____

_____ **6.** religion was important to the grandmother?

_____

_____ **7.** the author feels that the grandmother's employers did not give her the respect she deserved?

_____

► **Talk About It**
In this lesson, you have read about a mother handing down to her daughter values and skills that she learned from her own mother and grandmother. What are the most important things a parent can teach a child? What did you learn from your parents? What would you like to pass along to a child? Discuss these questions with your classmates.

Write About It: Write a Personal Essay

"Letting In Light" is filled with the author's thoughts and feelings. Now you will have a chance to write a personal essay in which you share your thoughts and feelings. First, study the sample.

Study the Sample

Read the steps below to see what the writer considered as he developed his essay.

Step 1: Picking a Topic. The writer chose to write about a place with a very special meaning for him—the home and property that have been in his family for generations.

Step 2: Developing and Organizing Your Ideas. To plan his essay, the writer made a chart of details he wanted to include, his thoughts, and his feelings.

Details	Thoughts	Feelings
• wide bend of shallow river • arc of land formed by bend • meadow with wildflowers		• peaceful
• old house: sagging front porch, hanging shutters, broken windows	• Some call it dilapidated, but I don't.	• dear to me
• great-grandfather, grandfather, and father born there • spent childhood and summers there	• family roots there	• feel connected to past • hold it dear
• inherited the land and house	• decided to fix place up and live there • knew it would take a long time	• willing to work hard
• told Millie of plans to fix up		• afraid she might think I was crazy
• proposed there and she accepted		• feel I have a future there • happiness

Now read the writer's essay on the next page. Then it will be your turn.

A Once and Future Home

There is a wide bend in a shallow river nearly 50 miles from the town where I live. Embraced within the arc of the river's path is a small, peaceful meadow filled with wildflowers. An old house—some would call it dilapidated—stands among them. Its front porch sags badly, its shutters dangle crazily, its windows long ago were broken. But it is one of the dearest spots on earth to me. It is the house where my father and my grandfather and his father all were born. When I was a kid, I'd spend summers there. Even when I'd grown older, I'd visit Grandpa every Christmas. And when my father died, I inherited the house and all the land from the road down to the river.

So I have roots in that patch of ground. But that is only half the story. I have a future there as well. It was on the bank of the river that I stood one evening last year with the woman I loved. I told her of my ambitious plans to fix up the old place and live out in the country, in that meadow, in that house. It would take a number of years and a lot of hard work—if all went well. Then, hoping she wouldn't think I was too crazy, I proposed. Would she marry me once I'd fixed it up? Could she wait? Would she want to leave her life in town and start a new life way out here with me? Millie looked at me and said, "I want two things, Daniel. I want to be your wife, and I want to work harder than I've ever worked before to help you make this home our home."

Next year, we'll be moving into that home.

Your Turn

A. Prewriting

Step 1: Choose one of the topics below, or use the list to help you think of another.

- the most important thing you learned from someone older
- a person, event, or place in your past that has special meaning for you
- your feelings on returning to your childhood home or hometown
- the one thing you would change in your past and why

Step 2: List and organize details, thoughts, and feelings. If you like, use a chart to help.

B. Writing

Now write an essay about your tie to the past and the thoughts and feelings it gives you.

 Tip Look at the ideas you developed during prewriting to see how they are related. Group related ideas together into paragraphs when you write.

▶ **Save your draft.** At the end of this unit, you will work with one of your drafts further.

Lesson 9 ▶ LEARNING GOALS

Strategy: Visualize
Reading: Read a story
Skill: Understand point of view
Writing: Write a narrative essay

Before You Read

The selection in this lesson is from a longer story about workers in an auto assembly plant. Most assembly lines have these features:

• Workstations are arranged in a certain order.
• A unit to be assembled moves from station to station.
• The unit moves at a certain set speed.
• Each worker performs one task in assembling the unit.
• When a unit reaches the end of the line, it is a finished product.
• Unskilled workers can learn their jobs fairly quickly.

How do you think it feels to work on such an assembly line day after day?

_____

Do you think teamwork among workers is necessary on an assembly line?
Why or why not?

_____

The story in this lesson was published in 1957, so some things about factory work have changed. Today, robots and computers do some of the work of putting together an automobile. But people are still needed to make sure the parts and the finished product meet quality standards.

Preview the Reading

Read the introduction and look at the illustrations. Think for a moment about the title of this story. Who do you think Joe is, and why is he a "vanishing American"? Look for the answers to those questions as you read.

Set Your Strategy: Visualize

Remember that it helps to visualize what you are reading about. When you visualize, you build mental images based on the details you read. You see in your mind the images the author is creating. As you read "Joe, the Vanishing American," try to visualize the assembly line where the men work. Picture what the men look like and how they act. When you finish reading, you will have a chance to describe what you visualized.

In this story, author Harvey Swados offers an inside look at the daily routine on an automobile assembly line in the 1950s. Through the eyes of Walter, a young man new to the line, you see the ways each of the other workers has come to terms with the job he must do day in and day out. You also come to see the lessons Walter is learning about life as a working man and about himself.

Joe, the Vanishing American

Harvey Swados

If Walter had not been so desperately anxious to go away to college he might never have been able to stick it out those first few weeks at the factory. His father, once district sales manager for a bankrupt sewing-machine concern, had come down in the world and was now a continually uneasy clerk in the branch office of a usury[1] outfit called the Friendly Finance Corporation; his mother, who had borne Walter late in life, clung jealously to the fading prestige[2] conferred on her by her many beneficences[3] on behalf of the Ladies' Guild.

Walter had never done anything harder than shovel the neighbors' snowy driveways and sell magazines to reluctant relatives. But the night of his graduation from high school his father grunted in a choked voice that there was no money to send him to college. Walter swore to himself that he would get a college education if he had to rob a bank. At the commencement exercise a classmate

had told him that you could get a job at the new auto assembly plant if you said on your application that you had worked as a garage mechanic. While his parents rocked creakily, proud but miserable, on the porch glider, Walter mounted the narrow steps to his little room and sat down at his desk. If he could work steadily at the plant for a year he ought to be able to save several thousand dollars even after contributing his share of the household expenses. Without saying a word to his parents, he went to the plant the following morning and filled out an application blank. Three days later he received a telegram asking him to report for work at 6:30 A.M.

. . .

His surroundings meant nothing to Walter, who had not expected that the factory would look like an art gallery; but the work, and the conditions under which he had to do it, were a nightmare of endless horror from which Walter sometimes thought, stumbling wearily out of the plant after ten hours of unremitting anguish, he would one day awaken with a scream. It was not simply that

---

1. **usury** (YOO/zhu/ree): the business practice of lending money at an extremely high interest rate
2. **prestige** (pre/STEEZH): high standing and respect
3. **beneficences** (beh/NEH/fi/sen/ses): acts of charity

the idea of working on an endless succession of auto bodies as they came slowly but ineluctably[4] rolling down the assembly line like so many faceless steel robots was both monotonous and stupefying, or that the heavy work of finding bumps and dents in them, knocking them out and filing them down, was in itself too exhausting.

No, it was the strain of having to work both fast and accurately, with the foreman standing over him and glaring through his thick-lensed glasses, that made Walter dread the beginning of each day. Under the best of conditions, he figured, he had three and a half minutes to complete his metal-finishing work from the time he started a job on his line to the time it reached the platform and was swung off on hooks toward the bonderizing[5] booth. If he began at the very beginning, as soon as the inspector had indicated bad spots with a stump of chalk, circling hollows and x-ing high spots, he could finish before the job reached the final inspector at the far end of the line—unless the dents were too deep or too numerous, in which case he was still madly pounding and filing, squatting and straining with the sweat running down his temples and his cheekbones while the solder-flower worked next to him in a tangle of rubber hose, melting lead and a blazing gun with a flame so hot that it scorched dry the running sweat on his face, and the final inspector stood over him, imperturbably chalking newly discovered hollows and pimples in the infuriating metal. Then he would straighten up from his hopeless effort and with a despairing glance at the impassive pickup man, who had to finish what he had left undone, he would hurry back down the line, praying to dear God that the next car—he did every third one—would be in fairly decent condition.

Worst of all were the times when he would hear a piercing whistle and would look up from the damnable dent at which he had been rapping blindly with the point of his file to see Buster the foreman all the way past the platform, waving angrily with his cigar. Hurrying from his unfinished work to his punishment, Walter would try to steel himself against what he knew was coming, but it was no use.

"You call yourself a metal man?" Buster would ask, stuffing the cigar between his teeth with an angry snap. "You want to get metal-finisher's pay and you let a job like that go through?" His eyes glinting with rage behind his thick spectacles, Buster would gesticulate[6] at one of Walter's cars, freshly speckled with chalk marks as it swung in the air. "Get going on it!"

And Walter would hurl himself at the job, dashing the sweat from his brow with the back of his gloved hand and filing away in a clumsy fury.

By the time he had somehow or other repaired what he had left undone, he would find on hastening back to the line that he was far behind once again in his regular work, so far behind that it might take him the better part of an hour to gradually work his way back on the line to where he really belonged, safe for the moment from shouted complaints.

Inevitably the men around him had suggestions as to how Walter might better his condition. Of the two other metal-finishers who worked on the line with him, one was a dour, fattish man, a leader in the opposition of the local union and disgusted because it did nothing to provide security for probationary[7] employees like Walter.

"I'll tell you something else. There's countries where a bright young hard-working fellow like you, that wants to go to college, doesn't have to waste the best years of his life in factory work just to save the money for college fees. He gets sent right through school and the government foots the bills. All he has to do is show that he's got the stuff and his future is secure."

---

4. **ineluctably** (i/ni/LUK/tah/blee): in a way that cannot be avoided or escaped; inevitably

5. **bonderizing**: coating steel with a special solution

6. **gesticulate** (je/STI/kyuh/late): make gestures, or arm movements

7. **probationary** (pro/BAY/shuh/ne/ree): concerning a time in which a person is watched and evaluated

Walter allowed that this sounded fine, although "having the stuff" sounded uncomfortably like his father's eulogies[8] of life in America, but he could not see what practical good it did him here and now—unless he was supposed to get satisfaction from the bitterness of knowing that in mysterious other countries his opposite numbers were better off than he.

The third metal-finisher, a lean efficient sardonic[9] man, had been listening silently to this talk of free college careers. He put his wiry hand inside his open-necked khaki shirt, scratched the coarse curling hair below his throat, and laughed aloud.

"What's the matter?" asked his fattish colleague suspiciously.

"You think your propaganda's going to change this boy's ideas about the other side of the world when everything here tells him he's got it so good?" He tapped the fat man on the shoulder with the butt end of his file as patronizingly as if he were patting him on the head. "Even if he has to suffer for his education in a way that shouldn't be necessary, he's free. He can blunder around and maybe even learn something that isn't listed in the college catalogues. Those poor kids you want him to envy, they may be getting their college for nothing, but they're paying a higher price for it than this fellow ever will. And the sad part is that most of them probably don't even know what the price is." And he turned back to his work without giving the fat man a chance to reply.

Fortunately for the three of them, the fat metal-finisher was transferred. He was only replaced, however, by an intense worker with two vertical wrinkles between his brows, who watched Walter's ineffectual work with growing impatience. At last he could stand it no more.

"In this game, kid, the knack of it is in the speed. The speed," he said fiercely, "and the way you concentrate on the job. If you're going to fumble around and just bitch about your mistakes, you'll be a long time getting straightened out." He greeted his own badly dented job, rolling toward them, with a smile of genuine pleasure. "Size it up quick, pick out the worst dents, and get going on them right away. Leave the high spots for last—the pickup men don't mind doing them."

The third man, the grey-haired cynic[10] whom everyone liked but no one seemed to know, had been listening quietly, with a strange, mild grin on his long and youthful face. He put a stick of chewing gum in his mouth, ruminated for a moment, and said: "What you really want is for him to enjoy his work, Orrin. Might be more practical if you'd get down and actually show him how to do it. Here, hold on a minute, Walter."

Walter had been squatting on his haunches before the wheel-housing of his job, blindly

8. **eulogies** (YOO/luh/jeez): speeches of high praise
9. **sardonic** (sar/DON/ik): mocking in a scornful way

10. **cynic** (SIH/nik): a person who believes all people basically care only about themselves

pounding with a hammer at his hidden screwdriver, trying hopelessly to punch a hole underneath so that with the screwdriver he could dig out a deep dent as the others did, trying so hopelessly that as he smashed the hammer against his left hand, missing the butt end of the screwdriver, he had to squeeze his eyes to keep the tears from starting forth.

"Give me that screwdriver."

Handing up the tool to the laconic[11] man, Walter noticed for the first time that he bore an unusual tattoo, faded like an old flag, on his right forearm: an American eagle, claws gripping his wrist, beak opened triumphantly at the elbow—you could almost hear it screaming. Without a word the man took the screwdriver and swiftly pressed it to a grinding wheel, fashioning a beveled point.

"Try it now."

Walter stuck the screwdriver under the car, rapped at it smartly several times—*bang!* it was through and resting against the outer skin of the car, just at the very dent. Gratefully, he turned to the grey-haired man, but he was gone, like a mirage.

There was something miragelike about him, anyway. He drove to and from work alone, he never engaged in small talk, he never hung around with a group at lunch hour or before work, he kept a paper book in the hip pocket of his khaki trousers, and always when he was not concentrating on his own work, when he was watching Walter or listening to the others handing him advice, he had that mocking irreligious smile on his long narrow youthful face. What was more, his cold blue eye seemed always to be on Walter, sizing him up, watching not so much his work, as everyone else did, but his temperament and his personality. It made him uncomfortable.

Gradually Walter began to sort out the other men around him, the ones who had more common reality in their talk and their tastes. Most companionable of them all was Kevin, the former

11. laconic (lah/CON/ik): using few words

rural school teacher, now an immigrant hook-man. His accent was so delightful, his turns of speech so happy, that Walter engaged the towering redhead in conversation at every opportunity.

"Hey, Kevin," he shouted at him one day, "how old were those kids you taught in County Kerry?"

"Ah, Walter," Kevin sighed, showing his long white teeth as he spoke, "they weren't *all* such children. If you were to see some of the older girls—quite well developed, they were. Oh, how shameful if they had known what was passing through their schoolmaster's mind!"

Kevin laughed at the memory, Walter at the picture the big fellow conjured up of countryside lust; he turned around and there was the grey-haired metal-finisher, smiling too, but so coldly you would have thought him a scientist observing a successful experiment. It was chilling, and yet not wholly unpleasant. In a way that he could not define, Walter felt that he was being judged and approved.

This third man, reserved and anonymous as ever, continued to observe him as Walter chatted not only with Kevin and the second metal-finisher, but with all of the other men on their line. Conversation was necessarily shouted and fragmentary, but Walter was astonished at how intimacies could be revealed in the course of a few phrases:

"A man's a fool to get married."

"Grab the overtime while you can. In the auto industry you never know when you'll be laid off."

"Happiest time of my life was when I was in the army."

"Only reason I'm here is because I was too stupid to learn a trade."

"I came here out of curiosity, but my curiosity's all used up."

"My wife says if I quit I'll have a better chance to line up a construction job."

"Walter, don't turn out like those college men who can tell you how to do everything but can't do a damn thing themselves."

. . .

One day the younger inspector at the beginning of the line, blowing genial clouds of illegal pipe smoke, gave Walter some frank and cynical advice.

"Been listening to the bosses talking about you, buddy." He took the pipe from his mouth and formed a fat smoke ring. "Want to know what's wrong with what you're doing?"

"I guess so," said Walter dully.

"You try too hard. You're trying to do a good job—that's the worst thing you can do."

Walter stared in bewilderment at the inspector. "But why?"

"They're interested in pulling production. If you're going to be running up and down the line all day trying to make every job perfect, you're just going to get in people's way. What the bosses will do is, they'll look for an excuse to fire you before your probationary period is up, or else they'll stick you in a routine lower-paying job."

"Then . . ."

"I've been here ten years. Believe me," he drew on his pipe once again and smiled disarmingly,[12] "they're not interested in making good cars, they're interested in making cars. You know what production means? Volume. And you know what they hired you for? To camouflage, not to get rid of every flaw. Hide them so they don't show up after the car's been through paint, so the customer doesn't see them at the dealer's, and you'll get along great."

"Camouflage them how?"

"With your sandpaper. With the grinding wheel. If you hit them up and down and then across, final inspection will never know what's underneath. Make it look good, and confusing. Be a camouflage artist and the bosses'll very seldom bother you."

Walter could not help laughing. "Listen, how could you stand it here for ten years? Every day I think maybe I ought to get out and look for something else."

"For six years," the inspector said pleasantly, "I was like you. This was going to be just temporary until I found something with a real future. It took me six years to realize that I was going to be spending the rest of my life here—it's like breaking in a wild horse, only with a human being it takes longer. I got married, had three kids, now I'm building a home near the plant. So I make the best of it, I take it easy, and I have as much fun as I can, and I hate to see a guy like you breaking his back all for nothing."

Bending over his work, Walter raised his file and heard the inspector's final shot, lightly enough intended but bearing its own weight of bitterness and resignation: "You'd be surprised how many fellows I've heard talking just like you, couldn't stand the work, going to quit any day, and now they're five- and ten-year men, starting to think about retirement benefits."

Walter could not clarify in his own mind what it was about the inspector's attitude that increased his desperation, not until his silent partner eased up to him from nowhere and said quietly, "Kind of terrified you, didn't he?"

"Not exactly terrified."

"Just the same, it's no fun to be doing time and to be told that your sentence just might turn out to be indefinite. Then if you've got a good imagination you can see yourself gradually getting used to it, even getting to like the routine, so that one day follows another and the first thing you know the wrinkles are there and the kids are grown up and you don't know where it's all gone to, your life."

Walter felt himself shuddering. Was it from the blower overhead that he felt his hot sweat turning cold and drying on his face? He said, "I suppose you have to be cynical if you're going to stay here."

"Day after day your life becomes a joke without any point, a trick that you play on yourself from punching in to punching out."

---

12. disarmingly (dih/SAR/ming/lee): in a way that wins trust

"But that's only if you're an imaginative or sensitive person."

For the first time, the man's angular face hardened. "Don't you think somebody like that inspector had his ambitions? Don't you think he still has his man's pride? Did you ever figure the cost of the job in terms of what it does to the personality of a clever intelligent fellow like him? He says if you're going to be trapped you might as well make the best of it, and by his lights he may be right. Anyway don't be too quick to blame him—he probably never had the opportunity to save money and go off to college."

No one had ever, not ever in eighteen years, talked to Walter in such a way. He would never again be able to look at a man like the inspector without compassion. Even at home in the evening with his father, whom he could no longer talk to about anything but baseball or the weather (although they both tried clumsily to broach other more serious topics), Walter found that he was viewing this desolate man not just as his father but as a man who had his own miseries; and this, he knew, was a part of growing up that could not have come about as it had without the influence of his strange friend in the factory.

▶ **Revisit Your Strategy: Visualize**

As you read the story, were you able to visualize the auto assembly line and the men who worked there? Write some details that you visualized.

_____

_____

_____

_____

After You Read

A. Comprehension Check

1. Before Walter worked at the auto assembly plant, he was a
   (1) garage mechanic
   (2) college student
   (3) finance officer
   (4) high school student

2. Walter started working at the auto plant in order to
   (1) shock his parents
   (2) learn a trade
   (3) save money for college
   (4) earn a living

3. Walter's job was to
   (1) identify faults in car bodies
   (2) knock out and file bumps and dents
   (3) solder metal
   (4) pick up what others had left undone

4. According to the young inspector, Walter's mistake was
   (1) trying to do a good job
   (2) wasting time talking
   (3) hiding flaws in his work
   (4) taking too many breaks

5. The inspector's comments bothered Walter because
   (1) he didn't think the inspector should talk that way
   (2) he was afraid he might lose his job
   (3) he was afraid he would end up the same way
   (4) he thought the inspector was lying

6. In the sentence "the final inspector stood over him, *imperturbably* chalking newly discovered hollows," *imperturbably* means
   (1) impatiently   (3) quickly
   (2) calmly   (4) impressively

B. Read between the Lines

Answer the following questions. Find evidence in the story to support your responses.

1. Later in the story, Walter's grey-haired "silent partner" tells Walter to call him "Joe, the vanishing American." Why do you think he says that?

   _____

2. Reread the last paragraph. What lesson did Walter learn from his "strange friend"?

   _____

   _____

C. Think beyond the Reading

Think about this story, and discuss it with a partner. Answer the questions in writing on separate paper if you wish.

1. What might have happened to the young inspector with the pipe if he had been forced out of his factory job early on?

2. Think about robots and computers taking over assembly-line jobs. What must have happened to many workers when such automation took place?

Think About It: Understand Point of View

"Joe, the Vanishing American" is told by a narrator from a certain **point of view.** The point of view is the relationship of the narrator to the story. It determines what the narrator tells you—what you as a reader learn, how you learn it, and who you learn it from.

A. Look at Point of View

When you read fiction, you will understand it better if you can identify the point of view the author has chosen to use. There are three main types of point of view: **first person, limited,** and **omniscient.** Most fiction is told using one of these three types.

- **First person point of view.** The narrator is one of the characters in the story. You read only what that character sees, hears, feels, and thinks. For example:

   I walked into the plant, not knowing what to expect. My first thought was, "Is this where I will be spending the next year of my life?" Several workers glanced up at me. One looked at me scornfully. Another seemed to have the worries of the world on his face.

- **Limited point of view.** The narrator is not a character but tells what only one character sees, hears, feels, and thinks. You see the other characters through that main character's eyes. For example:

   The young man walked into the plant, not knowing what to expect. His first thought was, "Is this where I will be spending the next year of my life?" Several workers glanced up at him. One looked at him scornfully. Another seemed to have the worries of the world on his face.

- **Omniscient point of view.** *Omniscient* means all-knowing. The omniscient narrator knows everything that all the characters see, hear, feel, and think. You as a reader do too. For example:

   The young man walked into the plant, not knowing what to expect. His first thought was, "Is this where I will be spending the next year of my life?" Several workers glanced up at him. One thought, "This kid will never make it." "Oh no, another young one," a second worker mumbled to himself. "I hope he's not after my job."

From which point of view is "Joe, the Vanishing American" told?

If you chose the limited point of view, you were correct. The narrator tells you what Walter sees, hears, feels, and thinks. You see the other characters through Walter's eyes, hear only what he hears, and know only what he thinks.

Tip When you read a story with a limited point of view, you very often have to make inferences about other characters' thoughts and motives from what the main character sees and hears.

B. Practice

1a. On separate paper, rewrite the following excerpt from a first person point of view, as if Walter himself were the narrator.

> ▶ Walter could not clarify in his own mind what it was about the inspector's attitude that increased his desperation, not until his silent partner eased up to him from nowhere and said quietly, "Kind of terrified you, didn't he?"

b. Now rewrite the same excerpt as if the narrator's point of view was limited to that of the grey-haired man, the "silent partner." Call him Joe. You will have to imagine Joe's thoughts and feelings first.

2. If the story were told with an omniscient point of view, would the somewhat mysterious "silent partner" be as mysterious? Why or why not?

_____

_____

3a. You have learned how to empathize with people you read about. Which character in "Joe, the Vanishing American" was easiest for you to empathize with?

_____

_____

b. How did the story's point of view affect your ability to empathize?

_____

_____

_____

▶ **Talk About It**

What do you think the rest of Walter's story will be? Will he remain at the auto assembly plant for the rest of his life? Find a job with a better future? Go on to college? Discuss what Walter's experience has taught him and how it may affect his plans for the future.

Write About It: Write a Narrative Essay

"Joe, the Vanishing American" is a story, or narrative. It tells of a series of events and experiences of a young man working in a factory. In this section, you will have a chance to write a narrative essay. You might write about an experience in your own life told from the first person point of view. Or you might write about an experience of someone you know told from a point of view limited to that person. First, study the sample.

Study the Sample

Read the steps below to see what the writer considered as he developed his narrative.

Step 1: Picking a Topic. The writer chose to write about a man's career decision. It is a true story about a family friend who taught the writer something about self-sacrifice.

Step 2: Developing and Organizing Your Ideas. The writer thought about the important events of the story and listed them in the order in which they happened:

1. Danny Meadows plays city baseball.
2. enlists and fights in World War II
3. comes home
4. gets married
5. gets job as steamfitter
6. plays baseball
7. is offered minor-league contract
8. turns it down to support family

Now read the writer's narrative essay on the next page. Then it will be your turn.

Your Turn

A. Prewriting

Step 1: Think about an experience that taught you a lesson about life. It might have happened to you, or it might have happened to someone else. Here are some suggestions:
- your relatives coming to this country
- the first days on your first job
- the birth of your child
- a trip you took
- a true story about someone you know
- a war experience

Step 2: List and then order the events. Note details that you want to include in your narrative.

One Man's Choice

When you hear about professional athletes demanding millions of dollars, throwing tantrums, and selling their autographs, you may shake your head like I do. You might also want to compare them with Danny Meadows, like I do.

Danny was a minor-league ballplayer in the early 1940s. Like a lot of young men during those war years, he put his life on hold to serve his country. He enlisted in the Marines and was sent to the Pacific to fight.

At the end of the war, Danny returned to Milwaukee, Wisconsin, his hometown. Like a lot of ex-GIs, he soon got married. He got a job as a steamfitter, but he continued to play ball part-time in a city league. Danny was a pretty good ballplayer—a solid catcher and a fair hitter. In fact, he was good enough to attract the attention of a big-league scout. The scout offered him a contract to play with the Chicago White Sox farm team in Texas.

Danny thought things over. He loved playing baseball, and he had once dreamed of being a big-league star. But Danny had also just learned that his wife, Joan, was expecting their first child. The minor-league contract was for $75 a month, and Danny knew that there was a good chance he would not make it in the major leagues. Besides, even if he did make it, major-league ballplayers didn't make much money back then. Many worked at regular jobs in the winter. Danny's job, on the other hand, offered him security and a steady income. He decided to give up his dream of being a major-league ballplayer to support his family as a steamfitter.

Perhaps the next time you hear of a million-dollar athlete who thinks only of himself, you will remember Danny Meadows—who did just the opposite. Danny is richer in many ways.

B. Writing

Decide the point of view you should use. Then write a narrative essay about your topic on separate paper.

Tip   Notice how the writer has added details about the main events. Notice too that the writer tells the story from a point of view limited to the man he is writing about, but he has added an introduction and a conclusion that show his own point of view.

 Save your draft. At the end of this unit, you will work with one of your drafts further.

▶ Writing Skills Mini-Lesson: Correcting Sentence Fragments

A **complete sentence** contains a subject and a verb and expresses a complete thought. It can stand alone.

A **sentence fragment** does not express a complete thought. It cannot stand alone. Fragments make it hard for readers to understand what a writer means because the thoughts are incomplete. Here are some common types of fragments and ways to fix them.

1. Fragment: Before TV was invented.

   As you learned in Unit 2, this fragment is a **dependent clause.** It has a subject *(TV)* and a verb *(was invented),* but it is not a complete thought. It does not make sense by itself. To make a complete sentence, you can attach this fragment to an independent clause. Remember to add a comma after the dependent clause if it comes first:

   Before TV was invented**, people amused themselves in different ways.**

   People amused themselves in different ways before TV was invented.

2. Fragment: Televisions and radios two hundred years ago.

   This fragment has **no verb.** It does not make sense without one. To fix it, you can make the fragment into a complete sentence. Add a verb and any other words needed to make a complete thought:

   Televisions and radios **did not exist** two hundred years ago.

   People did not have televisions and radios two hundred years ago.

3. Fragment: Invented in the 20th century.

   This fragment has **no subject.** Depending on the subject, *invented* **may not be a complete verb.** To fix this kind of fragment, add a subject and a helping verb if needed to make it complete. You may need to add some other words, too.

   Television and computers were invented in the 20th century.

   Many useful things have been invented in the 20th century.

   Scientists invented **many useful things** in the 20th century.

4. Fragment: Thomas Edison. One of our greatest inventors.

   These fragments have **related ideas,** but they are **incomplete.** To fix them, you can combine them by adding a verb and any other necessary words.

   Thomas Edison **was** one of our greatest inventors.

   Thomas Edison, one of our greatest inventors, **was responsible for many changes.**

Practice

A. On separate paper, add words to each fragment to make it a complete sentence.

Dependent clauses:
1. Before cars were invented.
2. Until Edison invented the electric light.
3. After the telephone was invented.
4. When television did not exist.

No verbs:
5. No cars, airplanes, or trains 200 years ago.
6. First the railroads, then cars.
7. Home entertainment on the radio before TV.
8. A TV in almost every home today.

No subject and/or incomplete verb:
9. Building highways all across the continent.
10. Bringing people closer together.
11. Instead of watching TV every night.
12. More time reading, telling stories, and visiting friends.

Incomplete related ideas:
13. The invention of the telephone. By Alexander Graham Bell.
14. So much business nowadays. Done by telephone.
15. Although some people still write letters. To relatives and friends.
16. Now e-mail in the computer age. Fax machines too.

B. On separate paper, copy these paragraphs, fixing all the fragments you find.

The house with many windows was built during the Victorian Age. Named for Queen Victoria. Who ruled the United Kingdom for 63 years. From 1837 to 1901. During that time, inventions such as the internal combustion engine, the telephone, and the electric light. Paved the way for the advances of the 20th century.

So many changes in the 20th century. Changes in transportation and communication. Jet planes and fast automobiles. Computers, compact disks, photocopiers, and e-mail. Changes in the way we live. Synthetic fabrics, plastics, instant cameras, frozen food, movies, and TV. Many changes in the field of health. New medicines cure old and new diseases. Insights into how diet affects our health. Eating better and living longer.

What about the 21st century? What changes do you think we will see?

Reading Review

Andrew A. "Andy" Rooney is a humorist and commentator who has shared his wit and wisdom on the TV show 60 Minutes *for many years.*

Where Are All the Plumbers?

Andrew A. Rooney

For the past few days I've spent most of the time in my woodworking shop making a complicated little oak stool for Emily.

I like the whole process of writing but when I get back there in my workshop, I notice that I'm quite contented. Yesterday I worked until 2:30 before I remembered I hadn't eaten lunch. It even has occurred to me that I could give up writing and spend the rest of my life making pieces of furniture that amuse me. Who knows? I might get good at it.

It's a mystery to me why more people don't derive their satisfactions from working with their hands. Somehow, a hundred or more years ago something strange happened in this country. Americans began to assume that all the people who did the good, hard work with their hands were not as smart as those who worked exclusively with their brains. The carpenters, the plumbers, the mechanics, the painters, the electricians and the farmers were put in a social category of their own below the one the bankers, the insurance salesmen, the doctors and the lawyers were in. The jobs that required people to work with their hands were generally lower-paying jobs and the people who took them had less education.

Another strange thing has happened in recent years. It's almost as though the working people who really know how to do something other than make money are striking back at the white-collar society. In all but the top executive jobs, the blue-collar workers are making as much as or more than the teachers, the accountants and the airline clerks.

The apprentice carpenters are making more than the young people starting out as bank clerks. Master craftsmen in any line are making $60,000 a year and many are making double that. In most large cities, automobile mechanics charge $45 an hour. A mechanic in Los Angeles or New York, working in the service department of an authorized car dealer, can make $60,000 a year. A sanitation worker in Chicago can make $35,000 a year. All this has happened, in part at least, because the fathers who were plumbers made enough money to send their children to college so they wouldn't have to be plumbers.

In England, a child's future is determined at an early age when he or she is assigned either to a school that features a classical education or one that emphasizes learning a trade. Even though we never have had the same kind of class system in America that they have in England, our lines are drawn, too. The people who work with their hands as well as their brains still aren't apt to belong to the local country club. The mechanic at the car dealer's may make more than the car salesman, but the salesman belongs to the club and the mechanic doesn't.

It's hard to account for why we're so short of people who do things well with their hands. You can only conclude that it's because of some mixed-up sense of values we have that makes us think it is more prestigious to sell houses as a real estate person than it is to build them as a carpenter.

To further confuse the matter, when anyone who works mostly with his brain, as I do, does something with his hands, as when I make a piece of furniture, friends are envious and effusive with praise. So, how come the people who do it professionally, and infinitely better than I, aren't in the country club?

If I've lost you in going the long way around to make my point, my point is that considering how satisfying it is to work with your hands and considering how remunerative those jobs have become, it is curious that more young people coming out of school aren't learning a trade instead of becoming salesmen.

Choose the best answer to each question.

1. The author makes furniture in his woodworking shop because
   (1) he needs new furniture
   (2) he does not make enough money writing
   (3) he gets satisfaction from working with his hands
   (4) he wants the praise of his friends

2. How are jobs that require working with your hands different today from similar jobs years ago?
   (1) They require more education now.
   (2) They are higher paying.
   (3) They are harder to find.
   (4) They are held in higher esteem.

3. We can infer that the author's friends praise him when he makes something with his hands because
   (1) they realize that working with your hands is difficult
   (2) his woodworking is very high quality
   (3) they want to make him feel good
   (4) they don't know how little skill it really takes

4. The author is puzzled that the most important factor in choosing a career today seems to be the
   (1) satisfaction the work gives
   (2) money the work earns
   (3) prestige the work has
   (4) product created by the work

Journalist Charles Kuralt interviewed pilot E. G. Whyte for a TV show. In the selection that follows, the words spoken by Kuralt provide background information for images on the TV screen. Dialogue from the interview begins with the speaker's name in capital letters. The italic text in brackets tells what was happening at specific times in the broadcast.

The Pilot *(Roanoke, Texas)*

Charles Kuralt

KURALT: At the age of eighty, Edna Gardner Whyte thinks back on all the men in her life. Almost every one of them was an obstacle. They stood in the way of what she really wanted to do, but she did it anyway. She became a famous flyer. Today, she has a hangar where most people have a garage—no thanks to men. Take the year 1926, for example.

EDNA GARDNER WHYTE: The first three instructors I had told me to quit—I was going to kill myself. I knew I wasn't going to kill myself. I knew that I could learn to fly. If a man could do it, I could do it. They didn't want to solo me. They would just keep riding with me, ride with me, and wouldn't solo me, and I knew I could do it. The day he got out of that airplane, I sang all the way around the airport and came in and made a beautiful landing. I was so glad to get rid of him.

KURALT: From that day to this, Edna Gardner Whyte has put in thirty thousand hours in the air, probably more than any other woman in the world—no thanks to men. One tried to turn her down for her pilot's license, though she had the highest score. Many turned her down for airline jobs, though she had the highest qualifications.

WHYTE: [*flying craft; flying it upside down*]: When I get down near to eighty-five, I pull it up like this and I get . . .
[*Sound of passenger moaning*]

KURALT: The man who is moaning in the background is CBS News cameraman Isadore Bleckman. He has just been put through a snap roll by a little old lady of eighty.

WHYTE: It's good for your veins; only two and a half g's. Want another one?

ISADORE BLECKMAN: Nope.

KURALT: Such flying has earned Edna Gardner Whyte a roomful of trophies. Almost every one of them reminds her of some insult from a swaggering male pilot, with a white scarf and goggles. There was Maryland in 1934.

WHYTE: They put up a sign: PYLON RACE. $300 AND TROPHY. And so I thought, oh, I'm going to enter that, 'cause I'd be racing against men. I've always wanted to race against men, so badly.

KURALT: They laughed at her. She went up in her Wright Whirlwind J65 Aristocrat and beat their socks off—took their money and their trophy.

WHYTE: Next year, the same sign came out again: SUNDAY AFTERNOON AT 3:00. MEN ONLY.

KURALT: She never got mad; she got even.

WHYTE: This trophy here is Las Vegas to Philadelphia. It was in 1958 and it was a men's race. I was the only woman in it. They knew they had no worry from me. I was no competition. But we flew the race and I happened to come in first.

KURALT: She has happened to come in first 123 times, judging from the trophies I could count and all the newspaper clippings with photographs of the pretty young woman in goggles. When Amelia Earhart handed her a trophy in 1937, she already had a lot more flying hours than Amelia Earhart had.

WHYTE: [teaching young woman]: Educate that hand to do that. Educate this hand to handle the throttle.

KURALT: At eighty, she teaches flying. And her special pleasure is teaching young women like thirteen-year-old Sonya Henderson, making it easier for them than any man ever made it for her.

WHYTE: People ask me, do you regret not having any children? And I'll say, well, I feel like my students and my pilots are my children. I hope I can continue. I want to fly until after I'm a hundred, I really do. I want to keep flying races.

KURALT: Beating men.

WHYTE: Beating men.

Choose the best answer to each question.

5. Edna Gardner Whyte's flight training was different from training given to men in that
   (1) her instructors helped her more
   (2) more was expected of her
   (3) she wasn't allowed to solo for a long time
   (4) she wasn't as strong as the men

6. From the detail "When Amelia Earhart handed her a trophy in 1937, she already had a lot more flying hours than Amelia Earhart had," we can infer
   (1) she had beaten Amelia Earhart in a race
   (2) Amelia Earhart was a well-known flyer
   (3) she had more trophies than Amelia Earhart had
   (4) she was a friend of Amelia Earhart

7. When Whyte flew in a men's race in 1958, the men "had no worry" from her because
   (1) she couldn't fly that distance
   (2) her plane wasn't fast enough
   (3) she had never won a men's race
   (4) she was a woman

8. Since Whyte's "special pleasure" is teaching young women to fly, we can infer that
   (1) she wants to help women avoid the prejudices she faced
   (2) she makes a lot of money teaching young women
   (3) it is harder to teach young women than young men
   (4) more women than men want flying lessons

The Writing Process

In Unit 3, you wrote three first drafts. Choose below the draft that you would like to work with further. You will revise, edit, and make a final copy of this draft.

_____ your comparison and contrast of situations, places, or people on pages 88–89

_____ your personal essay on pages 98–99

_____ your narrative essay on pages 110–111

Find the first draft that you chose. Then turn to page 176 in this book. Follow steps 3, 4, and 5 in the Writing Process to create a final draft.

As you revise, check your draft for these specific points:

Comparison and contrast: Have you included clue words that help your reader know when you are comparing or contrasting?

Personal essay: Have you made your related details, thoughts, and feelings clear in paragraphs?

Narrative essay: Are the events in time order? Does your narrative have a good introduction and a conclusion?

Unit 4 Taking Chances

Some people thrive on risk. They love to take chances—in games, in their work, in their hobbies, in life. Other people play it safe. They value what they have so much that they don't want to risk losing it. In this unit, you will read about people taking chances: a young man trying to build a career in the risky music business, a woman who risked her job to help her co-workers, and athletes and business-people who took chances in their careers and succeeded.

Before you begin Unit 4, think about your own attitude toward risk. How much of a risk-taker are you? What things are worth taking chances to achieve? What things are not worth the risk?

▶ **Be an Active Reader**

As you read the selections in this unit
- Put a question mark (?) by things you do not understand.
- <u>Underline</u> words you do not know. Try to use context clues to figure them out.

After you read each selection in this unit
- Reread sections you marked with a question mark. If they still do not make sense, discuss them with a partner or your instructor.
- Look at words you <u>underlined</u>. Discuss any words you still don't know the meaning of with a partner or your instructor, or look them up in a dictionary.

Lesson 10

LEARNING GOALS

Strategy: Imagine
Reading: Read a story
Skill: Understand characterization
Writing: Write a character sketch

Before You Read

The reading selection that follows is an excerpt from *Our Noise,* a novel by Jeff Gomez. The excerpt tells about a young man trying to get his first big break as a professional musician. Before you read, think about the following questions and write responses.

1. Do you think it is hard to make a living as a musician? Why or why not?

_____

_____

2. If you had a child who wanted a career in music or some other risky field, what advice would you give him or her? Would you encourage or discourage your child? Why?

_____

_____

_____

Preview the Reading

Read the introduction, and look at the illustrations. Then read the first paragraph of the story to get an idea of the setting, the tone of the story, and the kind of visit Mark is about to have with his parents.

Set Your Strategy: Imagine

You have practiced visualizing and empathizing. Both of these strategies require using your imagination. Imagination is a powerful tool. When you read the following story, let your imagination go! Use your visualization abilities to picture what you are reading. Use your ability to empathize to go as deeply as you can into the characters and their lives. Try to see what they see, hear what they hear, and feel what they feel. When you finish, you will have a chance to identify some things you imagined.

Mark Pellion has been traveling with his band. Now he has returned home.
As the following scene from the novel begins, he has gone to his parents'
house to return the van he borrowed for his road trip.

Our Noise

Jeff Gomez

Walking through the overgrown backyard, Mark spots his parents sitting in the Florida room,[1] having a drink. In his father's hands he recognizes the telltale scotch and can smell the sweet cherry odor of his pipe as it escapes through the plate glass doors of the added-on room. His mother, still dressed in her tennis outfit, is comforting herself with a white wine spritzer. Mark tries to stomp his feet on the red-brick walkway that he helped his father put in three years ago, so as not to scare them as he approaches, but they still jump a foot when he knocks on the window.

"You scared me half to death, son." His mother rushes to greet him.

"Sorry, sorry," he says, entering the warm room from the cooler night air.

"Are you feeling okay, dear?" his mother remarks as she steps back to examine him. "You look thin . . . and pale."

"No, no, no, Martha," his father finally acknowledges him, rising out of his deep leather chair. "He's not thin, just lean."

"Well, in any event, you're staying for dinner."

1. **Florida room:** a semi-attached room with walls made of screens or glass

His mother turns to leave the room.

"But I've got to be at—"

"Nonsense," she calls back to him. "It's too late. I'm setting an extra plate."

Mark awkwardly crosses the room and sits down on a hunter green couch with oak claws for legs.

"So, uh, how's it been going around here?"

"Fine, Mark, just fine."

"Good, that's . . . good."

"Son?" His father walks toward him and puts his face close to Mark's. "Remember our deal?" His voice is deeper than his son's and could be used as the voice of God for a cartoon.

"Deal?" Mark's voice cracks.

From the kitchen Mark can hear the rattling of pans, his mother putting dinner on the table. He hopes she'll return quickly because his father never lays into him when she's around. After all, you always have to keep up appearances.

"The deal." His words cruise on a slight scent of scotch.

"Oh, yeah, the deal. Sure, about how if I borrowed the van again that I'd have to wash it out and clean it, especially after Gary got sick that one time and threw up all over the—"

"No, not that. The job."

"Hmm?"

Mark plainly remembers the deal he had made with his father almost four months ago when he had approached him about using the van yet again, and this time for the longest stretch of use ever. His father was cool to the idea, as he had expected, and at first flat-out refused. It took a few weeks of protocol and careful negotiation on Mark's part to finagle[2] a deal. The final terms were that this would be the last tour his father underwrote. Mark agreed, saying that next time it would be different. "We have some big things happening for us, Pop," he had said in this very room fourteen weeks ago, in the throes of trying to convince him.

"Big?" his father had said gruffly. "Like what?"

"Like . . . getting a record deal. A *real* record deal, not like the one we have now where we have to stay up all night folding the covers. You'll see. One day I'll make a living off my music, and then you'll be proud."

Mark let the words sink into the blue pipe-smoke air and waited for the reply he had waited all his life to hear: *"Son, it doesn't matter to me what you do as long as you're happy."*

Instead of this he was treated to the usual patronizing barrage[3] of fatherly double-talk, cheap words of familial loyalty and supposedly "grown-up" responsibility.

"You're becoming a man now, Mark, and it's time to get a real job, to quit playing and get serious."

At the time Mark had wanted simultaneously to cry and to strike his father. How could he be so blind? So hurtful? Over the years he had never ventured into any of the clubs to see his son play his music, never even tried to think of what it meant to him, and yet he was constantly asking him to give it up for some mundane but stable job that would pay the bills, as if that's all that mattered in life.

"I'll make you a deal, son," is the way the pact began. "You can have the van one last time, and if you come back a success, with enough money to live on, with enough resources to support yourself and not have to come to the back door begging for scraps like a goddamn dog, and don't think I don't know about the loans Mother has been shoveling your way"—he pointed at him with the nibbled stem of his pipe—"if you come back from this trip a man, I'll forget all about ever trying to make a difference in your life."

"And if I don't?" Mark's voice creaked again. He felt ten years younger than his twenty-three.

"And if you don't"—the old man's voice was inscrutable,[4] as if he wanted his son to fail to prove his prognostication[5] correct—"Then you'll do as I say."

At that point most of the tour had been booked, and Gary, Steve, and he had already quit their jobs, the bridges of their former lives still smoldering. There wasn't enough in their strained budget for renting a van, and without one, there was no possible way to go on tour. So Mark rose out of the leather chair, crossed the room, and shook hands with his father only because he didn't know what else to do. Looking back it seems foolish, but at the time he was sure that this tour was going to make a difference in his life, that it was going to be a success.

On the road a few days ago, drifting back into town, he knew that his father had been right. He had failed, and maybe his father had been right all along. Gary and Steve kept prodding him in the back as he drove, slump-shouldered, wanting to know what was wrong with him as they slouched over the Virginia state line. . . . He had never told them about the conversation he had had with his father a week before the tour.

"The deal," his father now repeats, moving behind the bar to refresh his drink.

---

2. finagle (fuh/NAY/gul): to get by indirect, often tricky means

3. barrage (bah/RAHJ): concentrated fire of bullets or missiles

4. inscrutable (in/SKROO/tah/bul): mysterious; not able to be understood

5. prognostication (prog/NOS/ti/KAY/shun): prediction

"Yes, sir, the deal," Mark says like a zombie. "Okay . . . you win."

"Good." His father marinates the trio of ice cubes in a small pool of Glenlivet. "Why don't you stop by the human resources department at the college first thing Monday morning. Ask for Mr. Harrison." His father breaks into a devilish grin. "He'll be expecting you."

"Oh, Randall." His mother finally breezes back into the room and lays a hand on her son's sunken chest. "You haven't been laying into him again, have you?"

The three of them walk through the kitchen and into the dining room.

"Of course not, dear."

The cool night air slams against his still burning ears, and he imagines steam is coming off him as his anger dissipates.

He rams his fist over and over again into the open palm of his hand, where it lands with a leaden thud and not the wet-slap *smack* of flesh on flesh as it did in the movies.

"Why do I always let him get to me like that?" he asks as he rounds a corner. A pair of headlights approach him, and he feels like an escaping fugitive wandering in the middle of the street, so he heads for the shoulder. "Why?"

The streets are eerily dark as the tall pines sprouting up from the expansive trees block out any traces of moonlight and the absence of street lamps only cocoon the air further in a black shroud. Mark keeps stumbling over the exposed roots that wrangle their way out of the ground.

Once outside the gates of Tiger Bay, as if the place itself had a spell on him (which he always suspected), he begins to cool down. His anger and frustration drain away, and he begins to enjoy his walk. He speeds up, and it feels good to begin to hollow out his now full and solid stomach. His beat-up thrift-store boots do not provide the best walking shoe in the world, especially as the exposed leather heel digs mercilessly into his ankle and wears quickly through the shell of the bleach-weakened sock, slowly slicing each of the seven layers of skin. But still Mark's steps perk up. He begins whistling and marveling at the clear night sky.

Over the past few months he had always volunteered for the night shifts of driving. He told Gary and Steve he did this because he wanted to be a nice guy, that he would unselfishly take the night shift so they could rest and keep normal human hours while he would have to hibernate, sleeping during the day like a damn bear with a guitar. But the truth was that he liked to drive at night because it was less complicated; there wasn't any traffic, and it was usually all interstates and large main roads. It wasn't until around mid-day that a map had to be pulled out and routes from the highway to the small club they were playing that night had to be found. Mark wished that usually troublesome task on Gary or Steve, anybody but himself.

A pleasant side effect of his late-night shift was that he could use the quiet to think, dream, and wait for the ringing in his ears to subside. He would stare blankly at the night sky that was almost always crystal clear thanks to the icy autumn wind.

It's strange for him now to look up and notice

stars and constellations he was watching hundreds of miles away just a few weeks ago from the inside of the smelly, dirty van. How he wished to be home then, and now that he was, how he wished to be someplace else. He kicks at some loose rocks collecting near a drainage ditch, stones too big to fit through the steel grating, and he agrees with Steve that he never wants to tour like that again. He knocks one of the bits of gravel into the street where it bounces once and then hits the side of a car with a metallic crash. As he looks back to see if anyone has noticed the sound, he knows that staying here is no solution, either.

He starts fishing for his keys when he gets two blocks away from his house, thinking it will give him something to do since both the clear night sky and his own thoughts only depress him. He clutches his keys now that he's four houses away, and he has his arm outstretched, ready to find the keyhole with still a full hundred yards to go.

As Mark enters the living room, the red blinking light on his answering machine catches his eye.

"It's probably Laura." He groans, crosses the room, and presses the small gray PLAY button. "Great, now what?"

He kicks off his shoes and tosses his wallet on the kitchen table as he waits for the machine to rewind and then play his message.

"Uh, hello, I'm looking for a Mark Pellion?" an older, confused voice says, a voice that Mark doesn't recognize.

The confused tone in the caller's voice is due to the fact that instead of having the standard "I'm not home right now, please leave a message and I'll get back to you as soon as I can" message, Mark has a full minute and a half section of dialogue from one of his favorite cheesy movies, *Pandemonium.*

"Uh, anyway," the male voice, which sounds close to middle age, continues, "my name is Henry James, and I'm an A and R[6] man for Subterfuge Records here in Los Angeles. I read about you in *Alternative Press* magazine, and I've heard your single of the month on Sub Pop, and, well, I wanted you to know I'm going to stop in and see your show Friday night at a club called, I think, The Scene. I'll talk to you more then, okay? Bye."

The message ends, and an excited Mark is standing in a pool of silence. His heart is beating rapidly. Sweat is beginning to form on his forehead and underneath his arms. He glances down at the phone machine on the end table, marveling at the message he has just heard, as if it had been left by a Martian.

Wait a second. Did I just hear what I think I heard? Is my desperate mind playing tricks on me? Is this the break I've been waiting for or a sign that I'm breaking up? To confirm his sanity he presses the gray button again.

"Uh, hello, I'm looking for a Mark Pellion?"

Yes.

---

6. **A and R:** stands for "artists and repertoire." An A and R man signs musicians to a recording contract and works with them to produce records.

▶ Revisit Your Strategy: Imagine

Think about the following scenes from the story. Then for each item, check all words that describe how you imagined Mark felt, sounded, or looked.

1. When Mark first arrived at his parents' home, his mother remarked, "You look thin . . . and pale." How did you imagine Mark felt at the time?

_____ tired   _____ relaxed   _____ happy   _____ worried

2. When Mark's father told him of the deal he wanted to make, what did you imagine Mark felt at that time?

_____ proud   _____ respectful   _____ humiliated   _____ resentful

3. When Mark, "like a zombie," told his father, "Okay . . . you win," how did you imagine Mark said those words?

_____ angrily   _____ loudly   _____ softly   _____ without feeling

4. When Mark's mother "breezes back into the room and lays a hand on her son's sunken chest," how did you imagine Mark looked?

_____ happy   _____ defeated   _____ furious   _____ humiliated

5. When Mark is "standing in a pool of silence" after listening to the message on the answering machine, how do you imagine he felt?

_____ disbelieving   _____ electrified   _____ calm   _____ angry

After You Read

A. Comprehension Check

1. What did Mark promise his father he would do if the road trip was not successful?
   (1) give up music and get a job
   (2) go back to school
   (3) return to live with his parents
   (4) stop asking for support

2. Why did Mark make the deal with his father?
   (1) He was ready to quit after one last try.
   (2) He needed the van for the trip.
   (3) He thought he could talk his way out of it.
   (4) He realized his father was right.

3. Who is the message on Mark's answering machine from?
   (1) a fan
   (2) a girlfriend
   (3) a music reviewer
   (4) a record company representative

4. *Our Noise* is told from the point of view of
   (1) Mark's father
   (2) an omniscient narrator
   (3) Mark
   (4) a first person narrator

5. The tone of this excerpt indicates that the author
   (1) is annoyed with Mark
   (2) doesn't care what happens to Mark
   (3) is sympathetic to Mark
   (4) agrees with Mark's father

6. In the sentence ". . . he imagines steam is coming off him as his anger *dissipates*," *dissipates* means
   (1) sizzles   (3) expands
   (2) turns to steam   (4) goes slowly away

B. Read between the Lines

Check each statement below that you might infer from information in the story. Look back at the story for evidence to support each statement you check.

_____ 1. Mark is the leader of his group.
_____ 2. Mark's father expected him to succeed with his music.
_____ 3. Mark's father has browbeaten and dominated him in the past.
_____ 4. Mark's mother thinks he is going to be a star.
_____ 5. Mark's father does not think music is a worthwhile career.
_____ 6. Mark's group is definitely going to get a recording contract.

C. Think beyond the Reading

Discuss these questions with a partner. Answer them in writing on separate paper if you wish.

1. Do you think Mark has the right to expect financial support from his parents? What about emotional support? Should parents support their adult child even if they think the child is on the wrong track?

2. Look back at question 2 in Before You Read on page 120. Compare or contrast your answer with the way Mark's father treats his son.

Think About It: Understand Characterization

Characterization is the way authors create their characters. Sometimes authors describe the personalities, motives, and values of their characters directly. Often, authors reveal character traits by telling us what the characters say and do, how they look, what they think, and what others think of them. The reader must infer from such details the kind of person each character is.

A. Look at Characterization

1. Reread this excerpt from the story, and pay close attention to the details the author gives about Mark's father.

   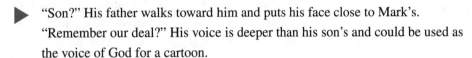 "Son?" His father walks toward him and puts his face close to Mark's. "Remember our deal?" His voice is deeper than his son's and could be used as the voice of God for a cartoon.

   "Deal?" Mark's voice cracks.

   From the kitchen Mark can hear the rattling of pans, his mother putting dinner on the table. He hopes she'll return quickly because his father never lays into him when she's around. After all, you always have to keep up appearances.

   "The deal." His words cruise on a slight scent of scotch.

   Consider the details "His father . . . puts his face close to Mark's" and "His voice is deeper than his son's and could be used as the voice of God for a cartoon." You can infer from these details that Mark's father intimidates him.
   The contrast between the father's deeper voice and Mark's voice that cracks suggests that there is an unequal struggle between them.
   Look at the details "his father never lays into him when she's around" and Mark's thought that his father always has "to keep up appearances." What kind of man "lays into" someone when no one else is around to see? You can infer that Mark's father is a bit of a bully.

2. Now consider the additional details in this excerpt.

   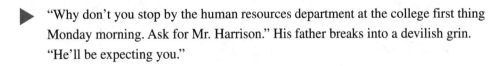 "Why don't you stop by the human resources department at the college first thing Monday morning. Ask for Mr. Harrison." His father breaks into a devilish grin. "He'll be expecting you."

   What do these details help you infer about Mark's father?

   _____

   You can infer that Mark's father enjoys bullying Mark and getting the best of him.
   You can also infer that he expected Mark to fail.

Tip You probably infer things about people you meet from how they look, what they say, and how they act. Use those same kinds of details when you read fiction to infer things about the characters.

B. Practice

1. Read the following excerpt. Then choose the *two* phrases from the box that describe Mark accurately. For each description you choose, write a detail from the paragraph that supports your choice.

> ▶ At the time Mark had wanted simultaneously to cry and to strike his father. How could he be so blind? So hurtful? Over the years he had never ventured into any of the clubs to see his son play his music, never even tried to think of what it meant to him, and yet he was constantly asking him to give it up for some mundane but stable job that would pay the bills, as if that's all that mattered in life.

is hurtful and mean-spirited	loves music
has a troubled relationship with father	makes practical plans

a. Description of Mark _____

   Detail _____

b. Description of Mark _____

   Detail _____

2. Read the paragraph on page 123 that begins, "A pleasant side effect" and ends, "icy autumn wind." Then choose the *two* phrases from this box that describe Mark accurately, and write details from that paragraph that support your choice.

a dreamer	wants everything his way
demanding	likes to be alone with thoughts

a. Description of Mark _____

   Detail _____

b. Description of Mark _____

   Detail _____

3. Character traits are also revealed by what a character does and how a character acts. Read these details from *Our Noise,* and write what you think they reveal about each character.

About Mark's mother

- "His mother rushes to greet him."
- "she steps back to examine him."
- She insists that he stay for dinner.
- She "breezes back into the room and lays a hand on her son's sunken chest."

a. What kind of person do you think Mark's mother is?

_____

About Mark's father

- "his father finally acknowledges him"
- "[Mark] was treated to the usual patronizing barrage of fatherly double-talk, cheap words of familial loyalty and supposedly 'grown-up' responsibility."
- "Over the years he had never ventured into any of the clubs to see his son play his music, never even tried to think of what it meant to him."
- "the old man's voice was inscrutable, as if he wanted his son to fail to prove his prognostication correct."

b. What kind of person do you think Mark's father is?

_____

About Mark

- "Mark . . . waited for the reply he had waited all his life to hear: _'Son, it doesn't matter to me what you do as long as you're happy.'_"
- "Gary, Steve, and he had already quit their jobs."
- "He had never told them about the conversation he had had with his father a week before the tour."
- "he feels like an escaping fugitive wandering in the middle of the street."
- "His beat-up thrift-store boots do not provide the best walking shoe. . . . But still Mark's steps perk up. He begins whistling and marveling at the clear night sky."
- "How he wished to be home then, and now that he was, how he wished to be someplace else."

c. What kind of person do you think Mark is?

_____

▶ **Talk About It**

In this lesson, you read about a father and son who disagree over the son's choice of a career. Discuss this situation from Mark's point of view and from his father's point of view. Role-play a conversation in which Mark and his father explain their positions to each other.

Write About It: Write a Character Sketch

The selection from *Our Noise* gave you a chance to understand the characters of Mark Pellion and his parents. In this section, you will have a chance to write a character sketch that will help a reader understand someone you know. First, study the sample.

Study the Sample

Read the steps below to see what the writer considered as he developed his character sketch.

Step 1: Choosing a Person to Write About. In the example below, the writer chose to write about his uncle.

Step 2: Developing and Organizing Your Ideas. A chart like the one below can help you think of and organize your details. Here is the writer's chart for his character sketch about his uncle.

My Uncle Otto

Category	Details
Physical characteristics	medium height; overweight; clean and pressed work clothes; shined boots; red suspenders; deep, slow voice
Personal characteristics	dignified; careful about appearance; trusted; concerned; makes people feel comfortable and important; always makes eye contact
Job	sells farm supplies; knowledgeable
Favorite activities	talking to people; playing poker

Now read the writer's character sketch on the next page. Then it will be your turn.

Your Turn

A. Prewriting

Step 1: Choose a person to write about—someone you know quite well and think others would enjoy reading about. Perhaps it is someone you love or admire. Choose a person from the list below, or think of one of your own.

- your husband or wife
- a family member or relative
- your boss or a co-worker
- a neighbor
- a friend
- your clergyperson

Step 2: Record details about the person on separate paper. If you like, make a chart like the one on this page.

Uncle Otto

My father's brother Otto has always been my favorite uncle. Otto is of medium height and more than a little overweight. His size, however, gives him a sort of dignity. People take him seriously, and that's important because Otto is a salesman. He sells feed and seed and other supplies to farmers. He knows about all the latest trends in agriculture. Farmers ask Otto questions, and they respect what he has to say. Otto has a way of talking slowly in his deep voice that makes it sound as if he is giving you very important information.

Otto dresses a lot like his customers, but not exactly. Otto's work pants and work shirt stay pressed and clean. Bright red suspenders hold up his pants, and his work boots are polished every morning.

Farmers like Otto. He comes to visit and even makes deliveries after hours in his own truck if he knows a farmer can't get into town. He'll walk into a barn to see a sick cow or out into a muddy field to look at how the crop is doing. Every customer is convinced that Otto is especially concerned about him. He makes people feel comfortable.

That's why Otto is such a devilish poker player. Everybody trusts him. And he can look you right in the eye whether he's holding three aces or coming up empty. For a man who is so careful with his business accounts, Otto doesn't let a bad hand stop him. He once bluffed his way to $100 with just a pair of twos!

B. Writing

Now, on separate paper, write a character sketch about the person you have chosen.

Tip Here are some categories to consider when you are thinking of details to write about a person: physical characteristics, personal characteristics, job, favorite activities, habits, accomplishments, skills, family, friends.

▶ **Save your draft.** At the end of this unit, you will work with one of your drafts further.

Lesson 11

▶ LEARNING GOALS

Strategy: Use your background knowledge
Reading: Read an article
Skill: Draw conclusions
Writing: Write an opinion essay

Before You Read

The following article tells how a woman risked her job to change the terrible working conditions in a fish-processing plant. She accomplished this by leading a drive to form a union.

1. Have you ever worked for an employer who seriously mistreated or misused workers? If so, what was the situation?

   _____

2. Have you or anyone you know ever been involved in an attempt to organize a union in a workplace? If so, what happened?

   _____

Preview the Reading

Read the introduction, the title, and the subheads. Look at the pictures. What do these features tell you about the article?

Set Your Strategy: Use Your Background Knowledge

To get the most out of what you read, use what you already know about the topic. Here are some facts about unions. List any other facts that you know about unions and about working conditions. Use this information to help you understand the article.

My Background Knowledge
- A union is a group of workers who elect officials to represent them with management.
- Unions are formed to increase the bargaining power of workers.
- Workers must vote to form a union.
- Union officials and management bargain over wages, hours, safety issues, and benefits.
- When bargaining fails, union members may vote to stop working and go out on strike.

_____

_____

_____

In 1985 a woman named Mary Young took a stand for herself and
her fellow workers at a fish-processing plant in Indianola, Mississippi.
They organized a union and fought for fair wages and safer working conditions.
Read about their struggle.

Work with Dignity

Charisse Waugh

PHOTO © 1997 BY REID HORN

Mary Young in front of Delta Pride, Inc.,
the factory she helped unionize to improve working conditions.

On a sultry morning in the Mississippi Delta in 1985, 29-year-old Oletha Brownlow was grimly focused on the razor-sharp knife blade embedded in the stainless-steel table in front of her. Every four seconds, she slid a catfish over the blade, tearing off the skin on each side and the back, for a total of 15 fish a minute. She and her fellow workers maintained this breakneck pace for up to 14 hours at a stretch, generating over 400,000 pounds of fish per day.

Supervisors holding stopwatches loomed over the 1,200 workers, who were mostly black women. The working conditions seemed out of another era: The machines in the cavernous room pealed so loudly that talking was impossible. The women were granted only six five-minute bathroom breaks a week and many were exposed to carbon monoxide from the trucks in the windowless processing area. There were no paid holidays. The average wage was less than $4 an hour, and there were no benefits.

Like many of her fellow workers at Delta Pride Catfish, Inc., Oletha suffered symptoms of carpal tunnel syndrome, a debilitating condition caused by inflamed tendons in the wrist. "I told my supervisors that my arms were bothering me," recalls Oletha. "But they said I either do that job or get fired."

Today much has improved for the workers, including increased wages, a pension benefits package and job rotation to prevent injury. The catalyst:[1] a young mother of three, Mary Young, who in 1985 took a brave stand to improve the lives of the women on the line.

The Promise of a Better Life

When Delta Pride opened its plant in Indianola, Mississippi, in 1980, it seemed a godsend. Until then, virtually the only way to eke out a living in the rural town was to work the cotton harvest part of the year, then do odd jobs or go on welfare for the rest.

In place of many of the cotton fields, the flat countryside is now broken up by ponds of green water, held in place by banks of soil. Each is stocked with catfish that is harvested every 18 months. Catfish is now the region's most valuable commodity,[2] and Delta Pride the largest producer.

"I had been on welfare for three years when the plant opened," says Sarah White, a single mother of two and Mary's good friend. "We thought it was our chance at a better life."

The women clocked in by 8 A.M. In between fish deliveries they were required to clock out but could not leave until all the deliveries had been made—meaning they were often on-site for more hours than they were paid for.

The harsh treatment at the plant offended Mary Young's quiet sense of what was just and fair. "I didn't like what was going on," she recalls in her syrupy Delta drawl, sitting in the neat-as-a-pin living room of her brick-and-frame house. It's a cozy domestic scene: Her 10-year-old son, Zetrick, sits next to his mother drawing while daughter Tusha, 15, juggles laundry and gossips on the phone. (Mary is separated from her husband.) "I knew these women couldn't take it much longer," says Mary, 40.

With her slender frame and serene disposition, Mary seems an unlikely person to take on the processing giant. She was raised in Indianola, and as a child, she helped her father chop cotton on another man's farm, while her mother drove a bus. She had never been an activist.

Her inspiration for change literally dropped from the sky. The United Food and Commercial Workers Union (UFCW) Local 1529 distributed informational cards from an airplane. Mary filled one out and mailed it back. "My husband's paycheck doubled when he joined the United Steel Workers," she said. "I thought maybe the same thing could happen for us."

Mary was the only worker who responded. Moved by her lone gesture, union officials sent a representative to her home. Mary vowed to recruit the 80 percent of workers needed for the union to hold elections.

Mary asked her friend and co-worker, Sarah White, to help. "I was afraid because I didn't want to lose my job and go back on welfare," Sarah says.

---

1. catalyst (KA/tul/ist): someone or something that makes an event happen
2. commodity (kuh/MOD/i/tee): something worth selling or buying

"But Mary said we could make things better." Motivated to build a decent life for her children, Sarah decided to help.

Fearful of putting anyone's job in jeopardy, Mary waited until after dark to load up her old Plymouth with sign-up cards and union brochures. She and Sarah would drive through the hushed streets of Sunflower County, dropping in on their co-workers in what became a yearlong campaign to win their allegiance.

The Fight for Fair Treatment

Management held meetings of their own, warning workers that a union would only pay for the luxurious life styles of reps, holding up snapshots of what they said were the snazzy cars of local officials.

Mary would attend those gatherings and strongly challenge everything management said. "She wasn't afraid of anything," says Bobby Moses, who was the special assistant to the Poultry Division of UFCW. "She had the ability to lead people."

Her hard work paid off. In October of 1986 workers filed into a plain white trailer at Delta Pride to cast their votes to unionize or not. It was a sight neither the workers nor management could have ever imagined.

"When we got ahead in the vote, everybody was hugging and crying," says Mary, laughing.

While they were celebrating, Delta Pride was preparing to go before an administrative judge at the National Labor Relations Board, calling the elections fraudulent.[3]

The judge sided with the union, and in October of 1987 the catfish workers at Delta Pride finally had a contract. The changes were revolutionary. Among them: A grievance procedure was established to allow workers to report abusive behavior; workers were no longer required to clock out when there were no fish to process; safety glasses and earplugs became standard gear; and a safety committee of union and management employees was created. And the women could spend Christmas, Thanksgiving and New Year's Day with their families and get paid for it.

There was still the issue of carpal tunnel syndrome, however. In November 1989 the union filed a complaint with the U.S. Department of Labor's Occupational Safety and Health Administration (OSHA) when 24-year-old Gloria Wilson was unable to work after she developed the disorder. "My fingers just wouldn't move," Gloria says.

OSHA fined Delta Pride $32,800 and ordered the company to redesign tasks and rotate workers to reduce the risk of injury as well as limit workers' exposure to carbon monoxide. Delta Pride appealed, then complied.

The atmosphere improved, but not for long. In 1990 the company offered workers a mere 6.5-cent-an-hour raise over each of three years. That

---

3. **fraudulent** (FRAW/juh/lunt): deceitful; false

September, the union called a strike, and with Mary leading the way, the women walked off the job.

It was the first labor strike ever in the Delta made up exclusively of black women, says Roger Doolittle, counsel for UFCW Local 1529. "It was the biggest strike in the country that year," he says. "Retail chains nationwide that sold Delta Pride products sent them back to the plant."

"It took lots of courage," says Dennis Mitchell, author of *Mississippi—A Portrait of an American State* and a professor at Jackson State University. "The Delta has a tradition of violence. There were almost no unions there." In fact, during the strike, there were several reported shooting incidents and violence on both sides of the line. By Thanksgiving, some women wanted to give up. "Just hold on, and we can win," Mary urged.

Throughout the strike, Delta Pride claimed economic hardship was responsible for the low wages. But finally, at the end of December 1990, the company settled with the workers, giving them a $1-an-hour wage increase and seven paid holidays.

Today, Mary is a supervisor at a competitor, Con Fish, and the management team at Delta Pride has turned over. The company's new president, David Spencer, welcomes the presence of the union. "We are working together to make a better environment," he says. Poverty still rules the Delta, and old ways die hard. But Mary is hopeful for future generations because she and the women she led fought for what was right.

A worker on a union-led strike in 1990. The union won.

▶ **Revisit Your Strategy: Use Your Background Knowledge**

Now return to the list in Set Your Strategy on page 132. Check each fact that was mentioned in the article. Include any facts you mentioned. Were any of the facts you added mentioned? Did you use the information in the list to help you understand the story of Mary Young?

After You Read

A. Comprehension Check

1. At first the Delta Pride plant was welcomed because it
   (1) produced good catfish
   (2) made use of land that had been cotton fields
   (3) paid taxes to fund welfare
   (4) provided needed jobs

2. Before the union, working conditions included all of the following *except*
   (1) up to 14-hour workdays
   (2) repetitive work that caused injury
   (3) sexual harassment
   (4) extremely low pay

3. Mary Young led the fight to unionize because
   (1) it was the only way she could become a supervisor
   (2) she didn't know what she was getting into
   (3) she hoped her pay would increase as her husband's had
   (4) she was a longtime union organizer

4. Carpal tunnel syndrome is caused by
   (1) repeated hand and wrist movements
   (2) moving the hands too quickly
   (3) working when the arms are tired
   (4) lifting and carrying heavy objects

5. Besides carpal tunnel syndrome, another condition that threatened Delta Pride workers' health was
   (1) loud machines in the cavernous room
   (2) no company-paid health insurance
   (3) carbon monoxide from trucks
   (4) no paid holidays

6. In the sentence "A *grievance* procedure was established to allow workers to report abusive behavior," *grievance* means
   (1) an accidental injury
   (2) a complaint about injustice
   (3) an unsafe condition
   (4) an unfair demand

B. Read between the Lines

Check each statement below that you might infer from information in the story. Look back at the story for evidence to support each statement you check.

_____ 1. Fish processing is now the main source of jobs in Indianola.

_____ 2. Before the vote on unionizing, workers talked openly about forming a union.

_____ 3. Delta Pride cared more about profits than workers' health.

_____ 4. Customers of Delta Pride supported the workers in their strike against the company.

_____ 5. Delta Pride could not give raises because it didn't have the money.

_____ 6. Mary went to work for a competitor because Delta Pride fired her.

C. Think beyond the Reading

Think about the reading, and discuss it with a partner. Answer the questions in writing on separate paper if you wish.

1. What do you think would have happened to Mary Young if the workers hadn't voted to form a union?

2. What qualities do people like Mary have that enable them to lead a fight for what they think is right?

Think About It: Draw Conclusions

When you **draw a conclusion,** you use clues in the reading together with other information you may have, just as you do when you infer something the author hasn't stated directly. To draw a conclusion, you come to a decision or conclude something based on your inferences.

A. Look at Drawing Conclusions

Reread the following excerpt from "Work with Dignity." Think about what conclusions you can draw from the clues in the description and your own knowledge.

> On a sultry morning in the Mississippi Delta in 1985, 29-year-old Oletha Brownlow was grimly focused on the razor-sharp knife blade embedded in the stainless-steel table in front of her. Every four seconds, she slid a catfish over the blade, tearing off the skin on each side and the back, for a total of 15 fish a minute. She and her fellow workers maintained this breakneck pace for up to 14 hours at a stretch, generating over 400,000 pounds of fish per day.
>
> Supervisors holding stopwatches loomed over the 1,200 workers, who were mostly black women.

What can you conclude from "grimly focused on the razor-sharp knife blade"? Using your knowledge of what a razor-sharp knife blade can do, you can conclude that Oletha's job was dangerous. And since she was "grimly focused," you can conclude she gave her job her complete concentration.

What can you conclude from the details "every four seconds," "15 fish a minute," "breakneck pace for up to 14 hours at a stretch," and "supervisors holding stopwatches loomed over"?

_____

If you combine those details with your knowledge of factory work and how important production goals are, you might conclude that Oletha worked almost continuously at a difficult, demanding job, under a great deal of pressure for long periods of time.

 Tip   Be careful not to jump to conclusions. Be sure your conclusion is justifiable and is supported by the details in the reading.

B. Practice

Reread each excerpt from "Work with Dignity." Then check every statement below it that is a justifiable conclusion drawn from the details.

1. ▶ When Delta Pride opened its plant in Indianola, Mississippi, in 1980, it seemed a godsend. Until then, virtually the only way to eke out a living . . . was to work the cotton harvest part of the year, then do odd jobs or go on welfare for the rest.

_____ **a.** Delta Pride opened a plant in Indianola because many catfish were caught there.
_____ **b.** Many people in Indianola lived in poverty.
_____ **c.** Delta Pride located in Indianola because the area offered cheap labor.

2. ▶ The United Food and Commercial Workers Union (UFCW) Local 1529 distributed informational cards from an airplane. Mary filled one out and mailed it back. . . .

Mary was the only worker who responded. Moved by her lone gesture, union officials sent a representative to her home. Mary vowed to recruit the 80 percent of workers needed for the union to hold elections.

_____ **a.** The UFCW pinpointed Delta Pride as a place where workers might need a union.
_____ **b.** Mary Young was the only worker who could read and write.
_____ **c.** Unless the majority of workers are for it, a union cannot be formed.

3. ▶ It was the first labor strike ever in the Delta made up exclusively of black women, says Roger Doolittle, counsel for UFCW Local 1529. "It was the biggest strike in the country that year," he says. "Retail chains nationwide that sold Delta Pride products sent them back to the plant."

_____ **a.** Delta Pride was unable to process and ship fish during the strike.
_____ **b.** There had been other labor strikes on the Delta, but they had involved male workers.
_____ **c.** The strike might have failed if Delta Pride's customers had not supported it.

4. ▶ Today, Mary is a supervisor at a competitor, Con Fish, and the management team at Delta Pride has turned over. The company's new president, David Spencer, welcomes the presence of the union. "We are working together to make a better environment," he says.

_____ **a.** Mary was fired from Delta Pride.
_____ **b.** The original Delta Pride managers were all fired.
_____ **c.** The new management team is working with the union.

▶ **Talk About It**
Discuss the reasons that Mary Young and Sarah White might have given another Delta Pride worker when they tried to persuade her to vote for the union. What were working conditions like at the plant? How might a union help change these conditions? Make a list of these reasons.

Write About It: Write an Opinion Essay

Mary Young had to persuade other workers to form a union. In her opinion, the union would help the workers. When you express an opinion, you state a belief. Supporting it with reasons can help you persuade others. Now you will have a chance to write your opinion. First, study the sample.

Study the Sample

Read the steps below to see what the writer considered as she developed her opinion essay.

Step 1: Picking a Topic. The writer chose to write about the pay at her company.

Step 2: Developing and Organizing Ideas. The writer started by stating her opinion. Then she used a chart to list her reasons, along with facts and examples she could use to support them.

Reasons	Facts	Examples
just as necessary to company's profits, if not more so	used to call on small or isolated accounts, now call on middle and large accounts too; responsible for more than half the sales	I call fourth largest customer.
more money available to pay us	cost the company less because we don't travel	
can give technical support much more quickly; increase customer satisfaction	are always a phone call away; know the technicians to call	James solved photocopying problem in half an hour.

Now read the writer's opinion essay on the next page. Then it will be your turn.

Your Turn

A. Prewriting

Step 1: Think of a topic about which you have a definite opinion. If you like, choose a topic from the list below.

- a current issue in health care
- a current issue in your community
- a current political issue
- a current issue in your workplace

Step 2: List ideas that support your opinion. Try to think of reasons, facts, and examples. Make a chart like the one in this lesson if that helps.

Inside Sales Reps Deserve More Pay

The company I work for sells office equipment all over the United States. My job title is Inside Sales Rep. Unlike field reps, who call on customers in person, I contact customers by phone to sell them our products. I think it is time my pay and the pay of the other inside sales reps match what the field reps have been offered for years.

Inside sales reps contribute significantly to company profits. We used to make sales to accounts that were too small or too isolated for field reps to call on. But there are fewer field reps now, so the inside sales reps call many middle-sized and even large accounts. For example, I call our fourth largest account. Inside sales reps are now responsible for more than half the company's sales. And we have helped maintain sales at less cost because we don't have travel expenses.

Inside sales reps offer better technical support than field reps. A field rep may be difficult to reach at a moment's notice. But when a customer calls an inside sales rep, we can immediately connect the customer with the technician here who knows about that piece of equipment. Just last week a co-worker of mine helped solve a photocopying problem that was holding up a customer's annual sales report. This kind of technical support increases customer satisfaction, which translates to even more sales in the future.

Customer sales, support, and satisfaction—the inside sales reps have contributed to all three, and, in turn, to the company's profits. Yet we are offered both a lower base pay and a lower commission on our sales than the field reps earn. We deserve to see our paychecks reflect our hard work and our contribution to the company.

B. Writing

Now on separate paper, write an essay in which you state an opinion and support it with reasons, facts, and examples.

Tip A good way to organize an opinion piece is to state your opinion in an introductory paragraph. Then use middle paragraphs to support it. Finally, sum up your opinion. Also notice that the writer's title states her opinion clearly.

 Save your draft. At the end of this unit, you will work with one of your drafts further.

Lesson 12

LEARNING GOALS

Strategy: Use your prior experience
Reading: Read an article
Skill: Identify problems and solutions
Writing: Write a narrative essay

Before You Read

The article in this lesson focuses on the importance of taking risks. The title asks, "Do You Risk Enough to Succeed?" Before you read the article, think about the following questions and write answers on the lines provided.

1. Do you think of yourself as a risk taker? Why or why not?

_____

_____

2. What is the biggest risk you have ever taken? Was it successful?

_____

_____

3. How do you decide when a risk is worth taking?

_____

_____

Preview the Reading

Read the introduction and the title. Skim through the article, and read the five numbered subheads. Look at the photos, and read the captions. Use these features to get a good idea of what you will be reading about.

Set Your Strategy: Use Your Prior Experience

As an adult, you have gathered a wide range of experiences. You can best understand and learn from a reading selection if you think of those experiences when you read. In the following article the authors use examples from sports and the business world. As you come to each example, think about similar experiences or situations in your own life. After you read the article, you will have a chance to compare your prior experiences with what you have read.

Playing it safe may keep you from failing, but it can also keep you from succeeding. Whether it's a game or real life, you sometimes have to take a risk in order not to lose your dreams. This article explains why.

Do You Risk Enough to Succeed?

Robert J. Kriegel with Louis Patler

CORBIS

Monica Seles, professional tennis player

During the semifinals of the 1990 Wimbledon tennis tournament, 16-year-old Yugoslav Monica Seles faced American Zina Garrison. As the match proceeded, it became clear that Seles's most formidable[1] opponent was not Garrison but herself.

"The match was so close," said a crestfallen Seles afterward. "I was going for the safe shots. Even on Zina's second serve I was scared to hit the ball for winners."

Garrison, on the other hand, didn't play it safe. "I just told myself to go for it," she says. "None of this tentative stuff. If I missed, at least I'd know that this time I went for it." Advantage, game, set and match to Garrison.

When things get tough, conventional wisdom tells us to play it safe, to pull in your horns. Consequently, rather than performing to our potential, we concentrate on minimizing our losses. As Seles discovered, the results can be catastrophic.[2]

Top performers in any field get to the top by confronting things they are afraid of. Cus D'Amato, the legendary boxing trainer, once said, "Heroes and cowards feel exactly the same fear. Heroes just react to fear differently."

1. **formidable** (FOR/mi/duh/bul): so great that it causes fear or anxiety
2. **catastrophic** (ka/tuh/STRAW/fik): terrible, disastrous

If you find yourself shying away from risks, these five tips will help you tap into the adventurous spirit buried in us all.

1. Take dreams seriously. We've all run into the seasoned veterans who have "seen it all" and always have reasons why *not* to do something. Before you finish a sentence they fire hose your great idea. Recalling someone who failed miserably trying a similar idea, these rescuers will try to prevent you from wasting time, energy and anguish on any new venture.

A manager for a major printing company recalled a talk he had with one of his bookkeepers. Her dream was either to become the comptroller of his firm or to start her own company. Although she hadn't finished high school and English was her second language, she was undaunted.

Out came the fire hose! The manager cautioned, "You do have good bookkeeping skills, but with your education you ought to set your sights on something more realistic." Angered by this, she quit the company to pursue her dream.

What did she do? She started a bookkeeping service for people who owned small companies and spoke English as a second language. Today, she has five offices in northern California.

The truth is, none of us knows what other people's limits are—especially if they have the passion, the dream, that makes them persevere[3] in the face of obstacles.

"The most important thing when you're starting out is not to let the naysayers steal your dreams," says Barbara Grogan, president of Western Industrial Contractors, a Denver construction and consulting firm. "The world is chock-full of negative people. They have a thousand reasons why your dreams won't work, and they're ready to share them with you at the drop of a hat. You just have to believe in your ability and make your dreams come true."

2. Take it in little steps. I learned the value of this precept[4] when I was a ski instructor, taking novices to a difficult slope. Going to the edge of the run they would look *all* the way down to the bottom. Invariably the hill would seem too steep and too difficult, so they'd back away.

To help my students overcome their fears, I would tell them not to think of skiing the whole hill. Instead, just try making the first turn.

This changed their focus. They were looking at what they *could* do, rather than at what they couldn't do. After a few turns they would become more confident and, without any prodding, take off down the slope.

The same approach can help you. When starting something new, don't focus on the whole task in front of you. Figure out a first step and make it one

---

3. persevere (per/suh/VEER): to persist in spite of opposition
4. precept (PREE/sept): a general rule or principle

you are reasonably sure of accomplishing. Lots of these little steps will eventually enable you to reach your goal.

3. Don't say "don't." At times, when facing a new situation, we rehearse our own defeat by spending too much time anticipating the worst. I remember talking with a young lawyer about to begin her first jury trial. She was very nervous. I asked what impression she wanted to make on the jury. She replied, "I don't want to look too inexperienced, too young or too naive. I don't want them to suspect this is my first trial. I don't . . ."

This lawyer had fallen victim to "The Don'ts," a form of negative goal setting. The Don'ts can be self-fulfilling because your mind responds to pictures.

Research conducted at Stanford University shows that an image in the mind fires the nervous system the same way as actually doing something. That means when a golfer tells himself, *Don't hit the ball into the water,* his mind sees the image of ball-going-into-water. So guess where the ball is likely to go?

Consequently, before going into any pressure-packed situation, focus only on what you want to have happen. I asked the lawyer again how she wanted to appear at her first trial, and this time she said, "I want to look professional and self-assured."

I told her to create a picture of what "self-assured" would look like. To her it meant moving confidently around the courtroom, using convincing body language, making eye contact with the witnesses and jury, and projecting her voice so that it could be heard from the judge's bench to the back door. She also imagined a skillful closing argument and a winning verdict. A few weeks after this positive dress rehearsal, the young lawyer won her first trial.

4. Make your own rules. Most successful people are mavericks whose minds roam outside traditional ways of thinking. Instead of trying to refine old formulas, they invent new ones.

When Jean-Claude Killy made the French national ski team in the early 1960s, he was prepared to work harder than anyone else to be the best. At the crack of dawn he would run up the slopes with his skis on, an unbelievably grueling activity. In the evening he would lift weights, run sprints—anything to get an edge.

Jean-Claude Killy

But the other team members were working as hard and long as he was.

He realized instinctively that simply training harder would never be enough.

Killy then began challenging the basic theories of racing technique. Each week he would try something different to see if he could find a better, faster way down the mountain.

His experiments resulted in a new style that was almost exactly opposite the accepted technique of the time. It involved skiing with his legs *apart* (not together) for better balance and *sitting back* (not forward) on the skis when he came to a turn. He also used ski poles in an unorthodox way—to propel himself as he skied. The explosive new style helped cut Killy's racing times dramatically.

In 1966 and 1967 he captured virtually every major skiing trophy. The next year he won three gold medals in the Winter Olympics, a record in ski racing that has never been topped.

Killy learned an important secret shared by many creative people: innovations don't require genius, just a willingness to question the way things have always been done.

5. Learn from your mistakes. No matter how much you prepare, one thing is certain: when you are trying something new, you *will* make mistakes. No writer, salesperson or athlete escapes failure, if he continually challenges himself.

In any walk of life, disappointments will precede success. As Walter Wriston, former chairman of Citicorp, said, "Failure is not a crime. Failure to learn from failure is."

When Jim Burke became the head of a new products division at Johnson & Johnson, one of his first projects was the development of a children's chest rub. The product failed miserably, and Burke expected that he would be fired.

When he was called in to see the chairman of the board, however, he met a surprising reception. "Are you the one who just cost us all that money?" asked Robert Wood Johnson. "Well, I just want to congratulate you. If you are making mistakes, that means you are taking risks, and we won't grow unless you take risks." Some years later, when Burke himself became chairman of J&J, he continued to spread that word.

By embracing risk, you will accomplish more than you ever thought you could. In the process you will transform your life into an exciting adventure that will constantly challenge, reward and rejuvenate you.

▶ **Revisit Your Strategy: Use Your Prior Experience**
Below is a list of the people used as examples in the article. Think about an experience you had with taking risks. Write a few sentences about it. Tell which example it most resembles and why. Share your experience with a classmate or your instructor.

- tennis star Monica Seles
- novice skiers
- skier Jean-Claude Killy
- printing company bookkeeper
- the young lawyer
- Jim Burke of Johnson & Johnson

After You Read

A. Comprehension Check

1. Monica Seles lost her tennis match because she was
   (1) crestfallen   (3) cautious
   (2) weak   (4) distracted

2. When you face a new situation, the authors advise you to
   (1) picture yourself succeeding
   (2) look professional and self-assured
   (3) make a list of do's and don'ts
   (4) plan for problems

3. Jean-Claude Killy developed a skiing style that contrasted with what other skiers were doing in all of the following ways *except*
   (1) the position of his legs
   (2) his position coming into a turn
   (3) the way he held his head
   (4) the way he used his ski poles

4. To succeed as Jean-Claude Killy did, you should
   (1) train very hard
   (2) try to find new ways of doing things
   (3) play it safe
   (4) focus on one small step at a time

5. When you challenge yourself to try something new, you will
   (1) refuse to be afraid
   (2) heed others' warnings
   (3) set sure goals
   (4) make some mistakes

6. In the sentence "Most successful people are *mavericks* whose minds roam outside traditional ways of thinking," *mavericks* means
   (1) people who don't like other people
   (2) people who don't go along with the crowd
   (3) people who prefer to be alone
   (4) people who try to harm other people

B. Read between the Lines

Check off each of the following sayings that the authors would probably agree with.
Find evidence in the article to support your answers.

_____ 1. If at first you don't succeed, try, try again.
_____ 2. A bird in the hand is worth two in the bush.
_____ 3. Never say never.
_____ 4. Be content with your lot; one cannot be first in everything.
_____ 5. The sky's the limit.
_____ 6. Better safe than sorry.

C. Think beyond the Reading

Think about the article and discuss it with a partner. Answer the questions in writing on separate paper if you wish.

1. Do you think the authors believe that you should always ignore advice? If not, how would they suggest deciding what advice to follow and what advice to ignore? What would you suggest?

2. Look back at your answers to questions 2 and 3 in Before You Read on page 142. Did anything in the article surprise you or change your mind? If so, what?

Think About It: Identify Problems and Solutions

A **problem** is something that needs to be fixed. A **solution** is what fixes the problem. In the article you read, the authors described some people with problems and explained how the people solved those problems. In general, these are the steps to solving a problem:

Step 1. State the problem.
Step 2. Identify the cause.
Step 3. Think of possible solutions.
Step 4. Evaluate the possible solutions, and choose the best one.
Step 5. Develop a plan to carry out the solution, and follow it.

A. Look at Problems and Solutions

Look back at section 3 of the article, which describes a young lawyer about to begin her first jury trial. Here are the steps to solving her problem as she might have expressed them:

Step 1. State the problem: I don't want to look as if this is my first trial, even though it is.

Step 2. Identify the cause: I'm very nervous about what might happen.

Step 3. Think of possible solutions:

   Solution 1: I can imagine all the things that could go wrong and try to prepare to avoid them.

   Solution 2: I can imagine what a positive performance would be like and try to achieve it.

Step 4. Evaluate the possible solutions:

   Solution 1: Imagining things going wrong may make those things happen.

   Solution 2: Imagining things going right might help those things to happen. Choose the best one: Solution 2.

Now complete the final step as the young lawyer solved her problem:

Step 5. Develop a plan to carry out the solution, and follow it:

_____

_____

The young lawyer's plan included these actions: (1) I'll picture myself moving confidently around the room, using convincing body language, making eye contact, and projecting my voice. (2) I'll imagine myself giving a skillful closing argument and winning the case.

Tip One way to evaluate a solution is to ask yourself, "Does this solution get rid of the cause of the problem?"

B. Practice

Reread the following story of Jean-Claude Killy. Then complete the steps that Killy took to identify and solve his problem. The first two steps are done for you.

▶ When Jean-Claude Killy made the French national ski team in the early 1960s, he was prepared to work harder than anyone else to be the best. At the crack of dawn he would run up the slopes with his skis on, an unbelievably grueling activity. In the evening he would lift weights, run sprints—anything to get an edge.

But the other team members were working as hard and long as he was. He realized instinctively that simply training harder would never be enough.

Killy then began challenging the basic theories of racing technique. Each week he would try something different to see if he could find a better, faster way down the mountain.

His experiments resulted in a new style that was almost exactly opposite the accepted technique of the time. It involved skiing with his legs *apart* (not together) for better balance and *sitting back* (not forward) on the skis when he came to a turn. He also used ski poles in an unorthodox way—to propel himself as he skied. The explosive new style helped cut Killy's racing times dramatically.

Step 1. State the problem: Although I want to be the world's fastest skier, I'm not.

Step 2. Identify the cause or causes: I haven't found a way to ski faster than the best skiers in the world.

Step 3. Think of possible solutions:

Solution 1: _____

Solution 2: _____

Step 4. Evaluate the possible solutions:

Solution 1: _____

Solution 2: _____

Choose the best one: _____

Step 5. Develop a plan to carry out the solution, and follow it:

_____

▶ **Talk About It**
Interview a friend or relative about taking risks. Ask:
- Did you ever take a big risk? Was it successful? Would you take it again?
- Did you ever decide to avoid taking a risk? How did that turn out? If given another chance, would you take the risk this time?

Discuss with classmates how people decide what risks to take.

Write About It: Write a Narrative Essay

In "Do You Risk Enough to Succeed?" the authors tell the stories of people and how they took risks to solve their problems and achieve success. Now you will have a chance to write a narrative essay telling about a risk. First, study the sample.

Study the Sample

Read the steps below to see what the writer considered as he developed his narrative essay.

Step 1: Picking a Topic. The writer chose to write about a risk he and his wife took by starting their own business.

Step 2: Developing and Organizing Ideas. The writer listed the events associated with taking the risk. He then numbered them in the order in which he would write about them.

1. My wife lost her job, and mine at greenhouse was nearly over.
2. Looked in newspaper and asked friends and relatives for news about jobs. Kept my eyes and ears open.
3. Customer walked into shop, needing office plants.
4. Started thinking of new office park and the demand for plants.
5. Decided to take the big risk of going into business on my own.
6. Got contracts with businesses for plants.
7. Negotiated with Baker family to rent and possibly buy greenhouse.
8. Have worked hard ever since!

Now read the writer's narrative essay on the next page. Then it will be your turn.

Your Turn

A. Prewriting

Step 1: Think of a time when you took a big risk. Or you might want to write about a big risk you decided not to take. Use the suggestions below to help you think of a topic.

- changing jobs
- getting married
- getting divorced

- moving to a new community
- standing up to an authority
- trusting someone

Step 2: List and organize your thoughts. Include the answers to these questions: (1) What led to your decision about taking a big risk? (2) How did taking the risk—or not taking it—turn out? (3) Would you do the same thing if given a second chance?

B. Writing

Now on separate paper, write a narrative essay about the risk you did or did not take.

A Growing Business

Last year, my wife and I found ourselves taking a big risk. We were scared, but everything is working out—so far!

In February, my wife lost her bookkeeping job. Just as suddenly, the owner of the greenhouse where I worked as manager died of a heart attack. His family announced that they were going to close the business because no one in the family wanted to run it. Things looked pretty gloomy. My wife and I read the want ads each day and asked everyone we knew about possible job openings. Then one morning, as I was hanging a Going Out of Business sign at the greenhouse shop, the door opened, and in walked the answer to my problems—though I didn't know it at the time.

The customer was an office manager whose company had just moved into the new office park on the edge of town. She was looking for potted plants to place in the reception areas and offices. "I don't know why I got stuck doing this," she said. "I don't know anything about plants. I'm sure in a few weeks they'll all be dead."

While I was helping her select her purchases, my mind was racing. Perhaps as many as a dozen firms had recently opened offices in the new office park, and there were several hundred more acres with construction underway.

That afternoon, I drove out to the office park. By six o'clock that evening, I had signed contracts with seven companies to rent plants from me and pay me a fee to maintain them. Within a week, I had worked out an agreement to lease the greenhouse and shop from the owner's family, with an option to buy.

This past year, I've been purchasing supplies, tending greenhouse plants, and traveling between the greenhouse and the office park to maintain them. My wife is kept busy serving customers in the shop and keeping the books. Things have been tough at times, but we are hanging on. Each month is a little better than the one before. And one day, we hope to be the proud owners of Greenery Row.

Tip You may find that a time line is the best way to organize your ideas for your essay. Or if you are writing about a risk that you took to solve a problem, you might want to use a five-step problem/solution outline, like the one in Think About It on page 148. Use the organizing method that works best for you.

▶ **Save your draft.** At the end of this unit, you will work with one of your drafts further.

▶ Writing Skills Mini-Lesson: Correcting Run-on Sentences

Writing complete, separate sentences helps make your ideas easy to understand. If you run your sentences together, your ideas will not be clear. A **run-on sentence** has two or more independent clauses run together without a connecting word or correct punctuation. Look at this example:

> **Run-on sentence:** They loved each other, they thought marriage was risky.

Here are three ways to fix a run-on sentence like the one above:

1. **Divide the run-on into separate sentences.** Each sentence will have its own subject and verb, begin with a capital letter, and end with a period.

   They loved each other. They thought marriage was risky.

2. **Join the two independent clauses into a compound sentence.** Use a comma and a connecting word like *and, or, but, yet,* or *so.*

   They loved each other, **but** they thought marriage was risky.

3. **Create a complex sentence.** Use a connecting word like *when, after, because,* or *although.* Place the connecting word at the beginning of the dependent clause. Remember to use a comma if the dependent clause comes at the beginning of the sentence.

   Although they loved each other, they thought marriage was risky.

   They thought marriage was risky **even though they loved each other.**

Practice

On separate paper, rewrite each run-on sentence in *two* ways to make it correct.

1. Marriage can be a big risk, some people never take it.
2. Pam and Glen got married they had been in love for three years.
3. Pam and Glen wanted children one day, they wanted to raise them together.
4. They decided to get married they thought about the risk of divorce.
5. About half of all marriages end in divorce they knew these odds.
6. Pam and Glen had had some disagreements, they had always worked them out.
7. They were willing to take the risk their love was strong.
8. They were married for five years, they started having serious problems.
9. Pam and Glen still loved each other neither wanted to risk divorce.
10. They went to a marriage counselor, they now believe their marriage will last.

Unit 4 Review

Reading Review

"One can resist an invasion of armies," Victor Hugo wrote, "but not an idea whose time has come." That is true in any field of human endeavor: the arts, the sciences, religion, government, business. The strength of a nation lies in its ideas, and nowhere is this more visible than in the American workplace, which has given new meaning to the power of a great idea.

Robot Helper

David Mazie

As Steve Roberts walked along the production line of the Ford Motor Co. plant in Lansdale, Pa., a small, slight woman with curly blond hair stopped him. "You say you want ideas," Florence Shuler said. "Well, look at this!"

Roberts was in charge of Ford's new employee-suggestion program for the Lansdale plant, and moments later he stood looking into a metal cabinet near Shuler's workstation. Inside were more than 42,000 thumbnail-size electronic parts, components of the computer "brain" in almost every Ford, Lincoln and Mercury vehicle. The parts had all been rejected by robots because the leads were bent. "That's ridiculous!" Shuler said. "On most of them, the wires are bent just a little. There must be a way to straighten them to avoid waste."

A materials handler and 34-year veteran with Ford, Shuler had not bothered offering ideas under Ford's old employee-suggestion plan. "Nobody paid attention to suggestions," she says, "and if they did, it took forever to get anything done."

Then in 1992, Ford launched the Continuous Improvement Recognition System (CIRS). It features a team approach to preparing suggestions.

Evaluation comes within 30 to 45 days, and winners receive "Ford Points" exchangeable for trips, Ford products and other prizes.

A few weeks after CIRS was announced, Shuler stopped Roberts and showed him the cabinet full of rejected parts. Impressed, Roberts urged her to form a team and prepare a suggestion. As her team, Shuler chose Ruth Hunter, 45, a parts-salvage clerk who worked alongside Shuler; Jim Himmelberger, 33, a manufacturing technologist; Bob Obold, 29, an assembly-line supervisor; and Bill Holnick, 62, manufacturing-engineering supervisor.

At the team's first meeting, Holnick summarized their task: "We've got to find a cost-effective way to straighten the leads so no harm is done to components or wires. And we've got to determine how much money we'll save by salvaging these parts."

During the next six weeks, the group came up with a die, or machine unit, that would successfully straighten 98 percent of the bent leads fed into it. Shuler worked with Hunter on cost analysis, Himmelberger designed the die, Obold did the testing, and Holnick coordinated and supervised.

In October 1992, Shuler submitted the team's proposal, which was approved in nine days. The team's die is now used to straighten leads on ten components. The plant's savings in 1994 totaled $215,000.

For the idea, Shuler and her team received "Ford Points" worth $10,000, or $2000 for each team member. Even beyond the financial reward, there was a bigger and more personal prize as well. "We saw how much we needed each other and how each of us could help the others," Ruth Hunter says. "It would have been impossible to do this without the whole team."

Choose the best answer to each question.

1. What was the problem at the Ford Motor plant described in the article?
   (1) defective robots
   (2) lack of leadership
   (3) basically good parts rejected as defective
   (4) low morale among the workers

2. What was Florence Shuler's first step after being asked to solve the problem?
   (1) She made a cost analysis.
   (2) She wrote a proposal for company executives.
   (3) She built a machine to fix defective parts.
   (4) She assembled a team to work on the problem.

3. What conclusion can be drawn from the experience at the Ford Motor plant?
   (1) Employees should not speak out.
   (2) It pays to encourage and reward good ideas.
   (3) Most employees won't work hard unless they are rewarded for it.
   (4) Robots cannot be counted on.

4. Based on Florence Shuler's actions, what kind of person does she seem to be?
   (1) complaining   (3) bossy
   (2) capable   (4) friendly

Dr. Frank Farley has spent 20 years studying what he calls "Type T personalities."
Big T types are risk takers; little-t types play it safe. Annetta Miller discusses
some of the possible explanations Dr. Farley and other researchers have found.

A Sensible Guide to Risk Taking

Annetta Miller

What makes some people rule breakers and others by-the-book traditionalists? Scientists believe that to a large extent the answer is in our genes. In a study comparing 70 sets of twins who had been separated at birth by adoption and 300 pairs who had been raised together, psychologist David Lykken and his colleagues at the University of Minnesota found that inheritance plays a significant role in how fearless we are.

The researchers asked each twin questions like, "Would you rather be in an earthquake or work for a week digging mud out of a basement?" Based on the answers, the Minnesota team concluded that genetic factors account for at least 40 percent of the differences in individuals' willingness to take risks.

Whether you love risk or hate it may be partly physiological, with roots in the central nervous system. One theory holds that people unconsciously seek to maintain a certain level of nervous-system arousal. Thrill seekers may have a higher arousal threshold, which they attempt to reach through stimulating pursuits—going scuba diving at the Great Barrier Reef, for example, or having a career such as risk arbitrage. It also may be that Big T types need more stimulation than others to get aroused. On the other hand, little-t types may be so sensitive that when faced with too much intensity, they retreat to safer surroundings, be it a quiet vacation spot or a secure career path.

The Gender Influence

In general, men are more apt than women to take physical risks such as hang gliding. Some scientists have hypothesized that testosterone—which men produce in much greater quantities—is the impetus for thrill-seeking behavior. However, studies are inconclusive, and researchers say that the hormone theory is unlikely to account for all the gender differences in Type T tendencies.

Cultural mores also play a big role. Women generally have been discouraged, even prohibited, from taking risks. In the business world, this couldn't be more obvious. "It's hard to be a risk taker if you're already perceived as being an outsider," says Muriel Vogel, Ph.D., a New York City human-resources consultant and a career adviser to women. "That's why a man will be more apt to say to his boss, 'I need $6 million for a piece of equipment,' while a woman won't be as likely to put herself out on a limb."

However, as women's role in society evolves, risk taking is beginning to achieve equal-opportunity status—at least in the non-physical arena. In 1986, Farley and colleagues screened a group of ninth-grade girls and boys for psychological traits ranging from creativity to delinquency, all factors related to Type T behavior. They found a striking difference in the way boys and girls manifested the behavior.

In girls, the Big T personality was associated with creativity and a willingness to take mental risks, such as trying an untested approach to a problem, or social risks, such as speaking up in class. However, in boys the trait most often showed up in the form of delinquent behavior—petty theft, vandalism and the like.

Choose the best answer to each question.

5. Which statement best expresses the main idea of this article?
   (1) Men are more likely than women to take risks.
   (2) Some thrill-seeking boys steal or vandalize.
   (3) Your approach to risk taking is affected by your genes and culture.
   (4) Understanding risk taking helps you become a smart risk taker.

6. What is one way in which males and females differ in risk taking?
   (1) Big T type girls are more likely to try a new way to solve a problem.
   (2) Big T type boys are more likely to be creative.
   (3) Men are less likely to take physical risks.
   (4) Women are more likely to have a higher threshold for risk.

7. Based on the findings of the study by Dr. Farley, you can conclude that
   (1) boys and girls have the same willingness to take risks
   (2) boys are more likely than girls to get into trouble with the law
   (3) all delinquency is caused by Type T behavior
   (4) girls need to learn to speak up more often

8. If low risk taking by women is seen as a problem, its cause is at least partly that
   (1) women are not as physical as men
   (2) women have not been in business long enough
   (3) girls are less creative than boys
   (4) girls traditionally have been taught not to take risks

The Writing Process

In Unit 4, you wrote three first drafts. Choose below the draft that you would like to work with further. You will revise, edit, and make a final copy of this draft.

_____ your character sketch of someone you know on pages 130–131
_____ your opinion essay on pages 140–141
_____ your narrative essay telling about a risk you did or did not take on pages 150–151

Find the first draft you chose. Then turn to page 176 in this book. Follow steps 3, 4, and 5 in the Writing Process to create a final draft.

As you revise, check your draft for these specific points.

Character sketch: Have you included details that help your reader picture and understand the person you are writing about?

Opinion essay: Do you state your opinion clearly at the beginning? Have you included reasons, facts, and examples to support your opinion?

Narrative essay: Have you organized the events? Do you tell how your decision turned out and whether you are happy with it?

Skills Review

This Skills Review will let you see how well you can use the skills taught in this book. When you have finished Units 1–4, complete this review. Then share your work with your instructor.

Reading Skills Review

Read each passage and answer the questions that follow.

People who have applied for a job may get impatient waiting to hear from the employer. Here's a look at the process from the employer's point of view.

The Employer's Viewpoint

Peggi Ridgway

Often there are several qualified applicants and only one job opening. The employer must narrow the field and select only one person. This is a tedious and time-consuming process.

The employer will consider the applicant's . . .

- Job skills and knowledge
- Number of months/years of experience
- Formal training/education
- Length of time on jobs (stability)
- Overall presentation in the interview and on the application/resume
- Initiative/motivation (demonstrated by work history and interview information)
- Enthusiasm/interest (shown in interview)
- Ability to work with others
- Verbal/written communication skills
- Ability and willingness to learn new methods and procedures
- Salary expectations

You may be absolutely sure that you meet ALL the requirements for the advertised position. And you may be right. What you don't know, however, may be that you are one of four people, ALL of whom meet ALL of the requirements. This is the point where the employer delves deeper into qualifications, calls additional references, confers with his boss or the department supervisor, and thoroughly evaluates each top candidate. This is a crucial point. An applicant with an edge on the competition—having more advanced training, additional experience in a related field, stability, a mature approach to the job and a glowing reference—will be chosen.

The highly qualified applicants may not necessarily be advised when the employer makes an offer to one of them. The employer does not want to disqualify candidates just yet—it's too early! If the offer is declined, someone else must be considered. This creates an in-between stage for the other applicants which can become frustrating.

Even top candidates get little or no news from some employers as the field narrows. Knowing the strategy—and reasons for these in-between stages—you can stay in the game all the way to the top.

What Do Those People Do All Day, Anyway?

While some companies have formal procedures for responding to applicants, including acknowledgments by letter or postcard, most do not. Many are minimally staffed. Even human resource departments, which address employment issues daily, devote their time to a large variety of other issues and are unable to respond to the dozens (sometimes hundreds) of employment inquiries they receive weekly. Company personnel are fully occupied with group insurance, retirement, payroll, discipline, training and attendance matters, to name only a few. It's a sign of our times that, in today's highly productive office there is little time for the courtesy of applicant acknowledgment.

Choose the best answer to each question.

1. What is the main idea of this article?
   (1) Final selection for a job opening can take a long time because often there are several qualified candidates.
   (2) Knowing what an employer looks for in an applicant can help you land a job.
   (3) Even highly qualified candidates may not hear from an employer right away.
   (4) Application forms and interviews are equally important in making a good impression.

2. What often happens because human resource departments are minimally staffed?
   (1) Qualified applicants do not know when the employer makes an offer to one of them.
   (2) Insurance, retirement, payroll, and other matters may be left undone while applicants are screened.
   (3) Only applicants who meet all the requirements are given interviews.
   (4) Even top candidates for a job may not hear from the company during the selection process.

3. Highly qualified job applicants who have not heard from an employer may make the mistake of
   (1) giving up on the job
   (2) thinking they are still being considered
   (3) contacting the employer
   (4) assuming the job is still open

4. From this article, we can conclude that employers seem to place the greatest emphasis on
   (1) professional courtesy
   (2) selecting the best candidate for a job
   (3) a quick employee selection process
   (4) developing a pool of qualified candidates

*You are familiar with Robert Fulghum as the author of "A Modern
Cinderella Story" on pages 77–78. Here he tells a story about a wise teacher
who took a chance on her students and how it paid off.*

A Different Kind of Cinderella Story

Robert Fulghum

A kindergarten teacher I know was asked to have her class dramatize a fairy tale for a teacher's conference. After much discussion, the children achieved consensus on that old favorite, "Cinderella." The classic old "rags to riches" story that never dies. "Cream will rise" is the moral of this tale—someday you may get what you think you deserve. It's why adults play the lottery with such passion.

"Cinderella" was a good choice from the teacher's point of view because there were many parts and lots of room for discretionary padding of parts so that every child in the class could be in the play. A list of characters was compiled as the class talked through the plot of the drama: There was the absolutely ravishing Cinderella, the evil step-mother, the two wicked and dumb stepsisters, the beautiful and wise fairy godmother, the pumpkin, mice, coachman, horses, the king, all the people at the king's ball—generals, admirals, knights, princesses, and, of course, that ultimate object of fabled desire, the Prince—good news incarnate.

The children were allowed to choose roles for themselves. As the parts were allotted, each child was labeled with felt pen and paper, and sent to stand over on the other side of the room while casting was completed. Finally, every child had a part.

Except one.

One small boy. Who had remained quiet and disengaged from the selection process. A somewhat enigmatic kid—"different"—and because he was plump for his age, often teased by the other children.

"Well, Norman," said the teacher, "who are you going to be?"

"Well," replied Norman, "I am going to be the pig."

"Pig? There's no pig in this story."

"Well, there is now."

Wisdom was fortunately included in the teacher's tool bag. She looked carefully at Norman. What harm? It was a bit of casting to type. Norman did have a certain pigginess about him, all right. So be it. Norman was declared the pig in the story of Cinderella. Nobody else wanted to be the pig, anyhow, so it was quite fine with the class. And since there was nothing in the script explaining what the pig was supposed to do, the action was left up to Norman.

As it turned out, Norman gave himself a walk-on part. The pig walked along with Cinderella wherever Cinderella went, ambling along on all fours in a piggy way, in a costume of his own devising—pink long underwear complete with trapdoor rear flap, pipe-cleaner tail, and a paper cup for a nose. He made no sound. He simply sat on his back haunches and observed what was going on, like some silently supportive Greek chorus. The expressions on his face reflected the details of the dramatic action. Looking worried, sad, anxious, hopeful, puzzled, mad, bored, sick, and pleased as the moment required. There was no doubt about what was going on, and no doubt that it was important. One look at the pig and you knew. The pig was so earnest. So sincere. So very "there." The pig brought gravity and mythic import to this well-worn fairy tale.

At the climax, when the Prince finally placed the glass slipper on the Princess's foot and the ecstatic couple hugged and rode off to live happily ever after, the pig went wild with joy, danced around on his hind legs, and broke his silence by barking.

In rehearsal, the teacher had tried explaining to Norman that even if there was a pig in the Cinderella story, pigs don't bark. But as she expected, Norman explained that *this* pig barked.

And the barking, she had to admit, *was* well done.

The presentation at the teacher's conference was a smash hit.

At the curtain call, guess who received a standing ovation?

Of course. Norman, the barking pig.

Who was, after all, the *real* Cinderella story.

Word of a good thing gets around, and the kindergarten class had many invitations to come and perform Cinderella. Sometimes the teacher would have to explain what it was about the performance that was unique.

"It has a pig in it, you see?"

"Oh, really?"

"Yes, the star of the show is . . . a *barking* pig."

"But there's no barking pig in 'Cinderella.'"

"Well, there is now."

Choose the best answer to each question.

5. How did the teacher solve the problem of the children wanting to choose different fairy tales to dramatize?
   (1) She chose the fairy tale herself.
   (2) She appointed a small committee to decide.
   (3) A child named Norman decided.
   (4) The children reached consensus through discussion.

6. Which term below best describes the author's tone in this piece?
   (1) critical   (3) ridiculing
   (2) humorous   (4) puzzled

7. Which term best describes the character of the pig as he was portrayed by Norman?
   (1) brave   (3) sympathetic
   (2) unconcerned   (4) bossy

8. Which of the following statements is the author's main point?
   (1) A kindergarten teacher let a child play a pig in a play.
   (2) A kindergarten class created an excellent play out of "Cinderella."
   (3) "Cinderella" is a good story for kindergarten students to act out.
   (4) Like Cinderella, a kindergarten student succeeded and got his due praise.

The graph below shows the percent of total payroll that temporary workers earned in various industries during 1991 and 1995.

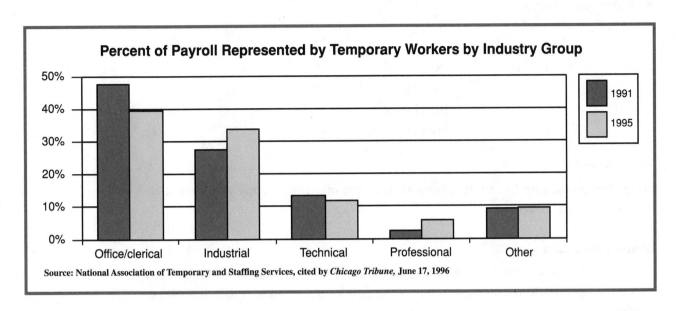

Percent of Payroll Represented by Temporary Workers by Industry Group

Source: National Association of Temporary and Staffing Services, cited by *Chicago Tribune,* June 17, 1996

Choose the best answer to each question.

9. In which two industry groups did temporary workers earn a larger percentage of payroll in 1995 than in 1991?
(1) office/clerical and industrial
(2) office/clerical and technical
(3) technical and other
(4) industrial and professional

10. Which industry group likely saw the most turnover in its employee rolls from 1991 to 1995?
(1) office/clerical   (3) technical
(2) industrial   (4) professional

11. In which groups did the percentage of payroll earned by temporary workers decrease from 1991 to 1995?
(1) office/clerical and industrial
(2) office/clerical and technical
(3) industrial and professional
(4) industrial and technical

Write About It

On separate paper, write about the topic below. Then use the Revising Checklist.

Topic: Do you think that people today have a harder time making a living than their parents and grandparents did? Or do you think it is easier today? Why? Write three or more paragraphs. Support your opinion with reasons and examples.

Revising Checklist

Revise your draft. Check that your draft
_____ clearly states your opinion
_____ includes reasons to support your opinion
_____ includes details or examples to explain your reasons

Skills Review Answers

Reading Skills Review

1. (1)
2. (4)
3. (1)
4. (2)
5. (4)
6. (2)
7. (3)
8. (4)
9. (4)
10. (1)
11. (2)

Write About It

Make changes on your first draft to improve your writing. Then recopy your draft and share it with your instructor.

Evaluation Chart

Check your Skills Review Answers. Then, on the chart below, circle the number of any answer you missed. You may need to review the lessons indicated next to that question number.

Question	Skill	Lessons
1	Identify the main idea	3
2	Understand cause and effect	1
3	Make inferences	8
4	Draw conclusions	2, 11
5	Identify problems and solutions	12
6	Identify tone	5
7	Understand characterization	10
8	Identify the main idea	3
9	Compare and contrast	7
10	Make inferences	8
11	Compare and contrast	7

Answer Key

When sample answers are given, your answers may use different wording but should be similar to them.

Unit 1: Getting Ahead

▼ Lesson 1

Revisit Your Strategy (p. 17)

Here are examples of thoughts and feelings Marilyn might have had: (2) She felt under pressure and alone. (3) Uncomfortable about going back again, she swallowed her pride to support her kids. (4) She is determined and has higher self-esteem.

After You Read (p. 18)

A. 1. (3)
   2. (1)
   3. (4)
   4. (2)
   5. (3)
   6. (4)

B. You should have checked 1, 4, and 5.

Think About It

B. Practice (p. 20)

1.

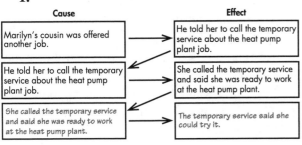

2.

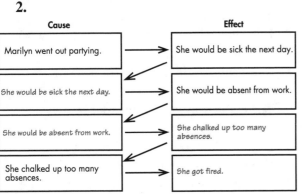

3.

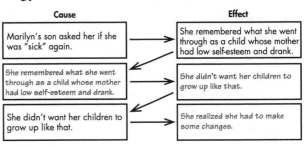

▼ Lesson 2

Revisit Your Strategy (p. 26)

1. While about **500,000** people used a union hiring hall to find a job, about **250,000** people were successful using that method. The success rate was about 1 in 2.

2. Of the almost 3 million people who asked relatives about jobs where they work, half a million people were successful using that method. The success rate was 1 in 6.

After You Read (p. 27)

A. 1. (2)
   2. (4)
   3. (4)
   4. (3)
   5. (3)
   6. (4)

B. You should have checked 2, 3, 4, and 5.

Think About It

B. Practice (p. 29)

1. c
2. a and c

▼ Lesson 3

Revisit Your Strategy (p. 35)

(3) is the best summary opening statement because it sums up the author's main message. Statement 1 tells only why you need to practice these strategies. Statement 2 is too narrow to be a general opening statement. Statement 4 does not mention any strategies.

After You Read (p. 36)

A. 1. (1)
   2. (4)
   3. (3)
   4. (3)
   5. (2)
   6. (4)

B. You should have checked 2, 4, and 5.

Think About It

B. Practice (p. 38)

Possible answers:

1a. Main idea of section: Overcoming your nervousness or fear can help you get a raise or promotion.

  b. 3 details:
- Don't be afraid to say you're qualified.
- An assistant manager missed chances to get promoted because he didn't speak up for himself.
- You have to work at letting people know what you want.

2a. Main idea of section: Being an "A" player can help you get a raise.

  b. Any 3 details:
- Raises aren't automatic.
- You probably won't get a raise if you don't perform well.
- It's more than okay to work hard and take on extra work.
- Be an "eager beaver."
- An assistant who gladly took on extra work got a promotion.

3a. Main idea of section: Use performance reviews to ask for a raise.

  b. Any 3 details:
- You often need a performance review to be considered for a raise.
- Before the review, list your strengths and accomplishments.
- Take this opportunity to tell your boss everything you've done for the company.
- If you've worked overtime, mentored, or volunteered, remind your boss.
- Take this opportunity to tell your boss what your career objectives are.

4a. Main idea of section: Have a backup plan in case you don't get a raise.

  b. Any 4 details:
- An office manager expected a good discussion, but her boss just said she was getting a 3 percent raise.
- Most raises are decided before you have your review.
- The amount of money for raises is often fixed, so if one person gets a big raise, another worker won't get much.
- If you don't get a raise, tell your boss you're disappointed.
- Remind your boss of your accomplishments and ask for another meeting soon to discuss a raise.
- One worker kept letting his boss know he was serious and ambitious and finally got a raise.

5a. Main idea of section: Finding a better paying job may be the only way to get more money.

  b. Any 3 details:
- Look inside your own company first.
- Apply for a job even if you don't have all the qualifications.
- A sales representative didn't get a job he applied for, but he started a plan to get a degree and be considered in the future.
- Seize every opportunity that comes along to show all your skills.

▼ Writing Skills Mini-Lesson: Compound Sentences (p. 41)

1. Kay liked to write about sports, and she had once interviewed Michael Jordan.
2. The newspaper was looking for a sportswriter, and Kay saw the ad.
3. Kay could ignore the ad, or she could take the chance.
4. She really wanted the job, so she applied.
5. The editor liked Kay, but he didn't want to hire a woman.
6. She knows a lot about sports, but the male athletes could be rude to her.
7. Kay showed the editor samples of her work, and the editor read them over.
8. The editor could hire Kay, or he could pass up a gifted sportswriter.
9. The editor was very impressed by Kay's work, so he decided to hire her.
10. Kay took the job, and she became a well-known sportswriter.
11. Kay got married, and then a few years later she had a baby.

12. Kay could stay home with the baby, or she could find a good child-care center.
13. Kay thought about quitting, but she loved her work and wanted to continue.
14. Her husband Fred decided to care for their child, so he quit his job.
15. Now Fred is a full-time father and home-maker, and he couldn't be happier.

▼ Unit 1 Review (p. 42)
1. (1)
2. (4)
3. (3)
4. (1)
5. (2)
6. (1)
7. (2)
8. (3)

Unit 2: Hard Times

▼ Lesson 4
Revisit Your Strategy (p. 50)
1. traveling musicians
2. a store selling supplies
3. food

After You Read (p. 51)
A. 1. (2)
   2. (3)
   3. (2)
   4. (1)
   5. (2)
   6. (4)
B. You should have checked 1, 3, 4, and 6.

Think About It
B. Practice (p. 53)
1. Possible answers: field turning frosty white, big wagons pull into front yard, cotton pickers load onto wagons at daybreak, remains of slavery's plantations
2. Possible answers:
   Tender Mornings
   • soft make-believe feeling
   • whisper and walk on tiptoe
   • odors of onions, oranges, kerosene

• wooden slat removed from door
• early morning air
• workers buying food items
• laughing, joking, boasting, bragging
• empty cotton sacks dragged over floor
• murmurs of waking people
• cash register ringing up sales
• sounds and smells touched by supernatural

Afternoon Harshness
• normal Arkansas life
• people dragging
• workers would fold down, dirt-disappointed, to the ground
• grumbles about cheating houses, weighted scales, snakes, skimpy cotton, dusty rows
• fingers cut by mean little cotton bolls
• backs, shoulders, arms, legs resisting further demands
• empty sacks left at the Store
• some sacks needing repair
• heavy knowledge the money wouldn't be enough
• harsh black southern life revealed

▼ Lesson 5
After You Read (p. 59)
A. 1. (1)
   2. (3)
   3. (1)
   4. (2)
   5. (3)
B. You should have checked 2, 4, 5, and 6.

Think About It
B. Practice (p. 61)
1. Possible tone descriptions include *calm, fearful, humble, reasonable.*
2. Possible tone descriptions include *forceful, irritated, pleading, proud.*
3. Possible tone words include *angry, demanding, desperate, forceful, frantic, pleading.*
4. The speaker's tone changes from being relatively calm describing his situation to being angry, desperate, and pleading.

▼ Lesson 6

Revisit Your Strategy (p. 68)

Mel was probably moving around with quick, agitated movements. His voice would be high, even squeaky, at times. Edna was probably more quiet, calmer at the beginning of the scene and more agitated toward the end.

After You Read (p. 69)

A.
1. (3)
2. (2)
3. (1)
4. (4)
5. (3)
6. (2)

B. Mel: 1, 2, 3, and 5   **Edna:** 3, 4, and 5

Think About It

B. Practice (p. 71)

1a. The company lost three million dollars. They closed the executive dining room. No one comes to work late anymore.

  b. The vice president has been using the same paper clip for three weeks. Nobody goes out to lunch anymore; they bring sandwiches from home and eat them over the waste basket. People are afraid that if they're not to work on time their desks will be sold.

2. No. He actually responds to only one of her questions—"Have they said anything?" Otherwise, he just keeps talking about the office.

3. concerned, disbelieving, and nervous

4. concerned and upset

5. She changes from being concerned and somewhat disbelieving and nervous to being very concerned and upset.

▼ Writing Skills Mini-Lesson: Complex Sentences (p. 74)

A.

2a. **Because** we had little money, we had very few choices.

2b. We had very few choices because we had little money.

3a. We'd be on the street **unless** we could find a place to stay.

3b. Unless we could find a place to stay, we'd be on the street.

4a. We stayed at a shelter **until** we found an affordable apartment.

4b. Until we found an affordable apartment, we stayed at a shelter.

5a. **Although** the new apartment was old and small, it was better than the shelter.

5b. The new apartment was better than the shelter although it was old and small.

B. Possible answers:

1. (When, Because, After) my husband lost his job, we lost our home.

2. (Because, Since) there was room at the shelter, we weren't on the street.

3. (While, When) we were at the shelter, it was hard to sleep at night.

4. There was noise and talking all night (since, because) the shelter was crowded.

5. (Since, Because) I like to cook, I missed being able to do my own cooking.

6. I was grateful for the shelter (when, as long as, because) it was all we had.

7. (When, After, Because, Since) my husband found another job, we moved into a small apartment.

8. (When, Whenever) I think about those weeks in the shelter, I'm grateful for our small apartment.

▼ Unit 2 Review (p. 76)

1. (3)
2. (4)
3. (2)
4. (3)
5. (1)
6. (4)
7. (3)
8. (2)

Unit 3: Then and Now

▼ Lesson 7
After You Read (p. 85)
A. 1. (1)
   2. (2)
   3. (4)
   4. (4)
   5. (3)
   6. (2)
B. You should have checked 1, 3, and 5.

Think About It
B. **Practice (p. 86)**
   1.

Then	Point of Contrast	Now
isolation	foreign policy and status	superpower
47 years	life expectancy	75.5 years

   2. Any three of these:

1890s Society's Rules	1990s Society's Rules
women's dresses covering ankles	women's dresses of any length
many topics of conversation forbidden	nearly anything can be mentioned
children addressed adults formally	children call adults by first name
children could be beaten for disrespect	many people frown on beating children
loveless marriages but few divorces	unhappy marriages lead to divorces

   3. Possible answers:

Before	Point of Contrast	After
women couldn't vote	women's suffrage	women vote
horses and mules	farm work	farm machinery
brutal job	housekeeping	household appliances
discrimination legal	civil rights movement	discrimination against the law

▼ Lesson 8
Revisit Your Strategy (p. 94)
   1. challenged, determined, and excited
  2a. engrossed and joyful
   b. pleased, glad, and proud

After You Read (p. 95)
A. 1. (3)
   2. (3)
   3. (4)
   4. (2)
   5. (1)
   6. (4)
B. You should have checked 1, 2, 5, and 7.

Think About It
B. **Practice (p. 96)**
   1. Yes. She worked as a maid for a rich, stylish redhead.
   2. No. There is no evidence that she got no help at home.
   3. Yes. Her dead husband left her with five children to support.
   4. Yes. She describes all the hard work her grandmother did for her family and her employer "until she was nearly 80."
   5. No. There is no evidence for this.
   6. Yes. Her children went to church and sang hymns.
   7. Yes. The author notes that the employers called her grandmother by her first name only, even though she was older.

▼ Lesson 9
Revisit Your Strategy (p. 106)
Some of the details you might have visualized include drills, saws, sanders, and other hand tools for working on metal; unpainted auto bodies sliding steadily along on a conveyor belt or on rollers; loud banging and grinding noises; dirt and dust; bright overhead lights shining on the auto bodies; workers dressed in soiled clothes, aprons, or coveralls, and perhaps wearing dust masks, goggles, and heavy gloves.

After You Read (p. 107)

A. 1. (4)
2. (3)
3. (2)
4. (1)
5. (3)
6. (2)

B. Possible answers:
1. Answers will vary. Support your answer with evidence from the story.
2. Walter learned to see people, particularly older people, in a new way—with compassion—and he probably would not have learned that lesson in college.

Think About It

B. Practice (p. 109)

1a. Sample rewritten from Walter's point of view:

I could not clarify in my own mind what it was about the inspector's attitude that increased my desperation, not until my silent partner eased up to me from nowhere and said quietly, "Kind of terrified you, didn't he?"

b. Sample rewritten with the point of view limited to Joe:

Joe looked at Walter. The young man had a look of uncertainty and even desperation on his face. Joe knew exactly what Walter was thinking. He eased up to Walter from where he stood and said quietly, "Kind of terrified you, didn't he?"

2. No, because we would be told this character's thoughts and feelings.

3a. You probably felt Walter was easiest to empathize with.

b. Because the story was told from a point of view limited to Walter, readers learned only his thoughts and feelings.

▼ Writing Skills Mini-Lesson: Correcting Sentence Fragments (p. 112)

Practice

A. There are different ways to correct the fragments. Here are some suggestions.

Dependent clauses:
1. Before cars were invented, **travel was much slower than it is today.**
2. **People used oil or kerosene lamps** until Edison invented the electric light.
3. After the telephone was invented, **communicating from a distance was easier.**
4. **People had other ways to entertain themselves** when television did not exist.

No verbs:
5. **There were** no cars, airplanes, or trains 200 years ago.
6. First **came** the railroads, then cars.
7. Home entertainment on the radio **came** before TV.
8. **There is** a TV in almost every home today.

No subject and/or incomplete verb:
9. Highways **have been built** all across the continent.
10. **Highways are** bringing people closer together.
11. **People used to read** instead of watching TV every night.
12. **People spent** more time reading, telling stories, and visiting friends.

Incomplete related ideas:
13. The invention of the telephone by Alexander Graham Bell **changed people's lives.**
14. So much business nowadays **is** done by telephone.
15. Although some people still write letters to relatives and friends, **most use the telephone.**
16. Now **we have** e-mail in the computer age and fax machines too.

B. Here is one way to fix the fragments. You may have used other ways.

The house with many windows was built during the Victorian Age. **The Victorian Age was** named for Queen Victoria, **who** ruled the United Kingdom for 63 years, **from** 1837 to 1901. During that time, inventions such as the internal combustion engine, the telephone, and the electric light **paved** the way for the advances of the 20th century.

So many changes **have taken place** in the 20th century. **There have been** changes in transportation and communication. **Now we have** jet planes and fast automobiles, computers, compact disks, photocopiers, and e-mail. **There have been** changes in the way we live. **Such things as** synthetic fabrics, plastics, instant cameras, frozen food, movies, and TV **did not exist before.** Many changes **have taken place** in the field of health. New medicines cure old and new diseases. **We have gained** insights into how diet affects our health, **so people are eating** better and living longer.

Think about the 21st century. What changes do you think we will see?

▼ Unit Review (p. 114)

1. (3)
2. (2)
3. (1)
4. (3)
5. (3)
6. (2)
7. (4)
8. (1)

Unit 4: Taking Chances

▼ Lesson 10

Revisit Your Strategy (p. 125)

1. tired and worried
2. humiliated and resentful
3. softly and without feeling
4. defeated and humiliated
5. outwardly calm but inwardly electrified and disbelieving

After You Read (p. 126)

A. 1. (1)
   2. (2)
   3. (4)
   4. (3)
   5. (3)
   6. (4)
B. You should have checked 1, 3, and 5.

Think About It
B. Practice (p. 128)
Sample answers:
1a. **Description:** has a troubled relationship with father
   Any 1 Detail: wants to strike his father; father never tried to think of what music means to him; father never went to a club to see Mark play
 b. **Description:** loves music
   Any 1 Detail: has played in clubs; father never tried to think of what music means to him
2a. **Description:** a dreamer
   Detail: uses the quiet to think and dream
 b. **Description:** likes to be alone with thoughts
   Detail: thinks it's pleasant to be the only one awake at night
3a. Mark's mother loves Mark and still wants to look after him. She probably still thinks of him as a small boy.
 b. Mark's father enjoys dominating Mark and shows no interest in what Mark cares about or feels.
 c. Mark wishes his parents understood him. He is unsure of himself and his future, but he is willing to take risks and to sacrifice for his music.

▼ Lesson 11

Revisit Your Strategy (p. 136)

Each fact that was in the printed list was mentioned or referred to in the article.

After You Read (p. 137)

A. 1. (4)
   2. (3)
   3. (3)
   4. (1)
   5. (3)
   6. (2)
B. You should have checked 1, 3, and 4.

Think About It
B. Practice (p. 138)

1. b and c   3. b and c
2. a and c   4. c

▼ Lesson 12
After You Read (p. 147)
A. **1.** (3)

   2. (1)

   3. (3)

   4. (2)

   5. (4)

   6. (2)

B. You should have checked 1, 3, and 5.

Think About It
B. Practice (p. 149)

Step 3. Think of possible solutions:

Solution 1: Work harder than everyone else (run up the slopes with my skis on, lift weights, run sprints to gain strength).

Solution 2: Develop new skiing techniques that no one else uses.

Step 4. Evaluate the possible solutions:

Solution 1: All the other team members are working hard and long too. This won't give me a competitive edge.

Solution 2: If I develop a technique that no one else uses, it will give me a better chance to win.

   Choose the best one: I will try to develop a new, faster technique.

Step 5. Develop a plan to carry out the solution and follow it:

Each week I will break one of the "rules" of current skiing technique until I find better ways to ski faster.

▼ Writing Skills Mini-Lesson: Correcting Run-on Sentences (p. 152)

There are different ways to correct the run-ons. Here are some suggestions.

 1. Marriage can be a big risk. **S**ome people never take it.

    Because marriage can be a big risk, some people never take it.

 2. Pam and Glen got married. **T**hey had been in love for three years.

    When Pam and Glen got married, they had been in love for three years.

 3. Pam and Glen wanted children one day. **T**hey wanted to raise them together.

Pam and Glen wanted children one day, **and** they wanted to raise them together.

 4. **Before** they decided to get married, they thought about the risk of divorce.

    They decided to get married, **but** they thought about the risk of divorce.

 5. About half of all marriages end in divorce. **T**hey knew these odds.

    About half of all marriages end in divorce, **and** they knew these odds.

 6. Pam and Glen had had some disagreements, **but** they had always worked them out.

    Although Pam and Glen had had some disagreements, they had always worked them out.

 7. They were willing to take the risk **because** their love was strong.

    Their love was strong, **so** they were willing to take the risk.

 8. They were married for five years **when** they started having serious problems.

    After they were married for five years, they started having serious problems.

 9. Pam and Glen still loved each other, **and** neither wanted to risk divorce.

    Because Pam and Glen still loved each other, neither wanted to risk divorce.

10. **Because** they went to a marriage counselor, they now believe their marriage will last.

    They went to a marriage counselor, **and** they now believe their marriage will last.

▼ Unit 4 Review (p. 153)
1. (3)

2. (4)

3. (2)

4. (2)

5. (3)

6. (1)

7. (2)

8. (4)

Writing Skills

This section lists the rules you learned in the Writing Skills Mini-Lessons in this book and other information you may find useful when you write.

Writing Compound Sentences

A **compound sentence** has two or more complete thoughts usually joined by one of these connecting words: *and, but, or, so,* or *yet.* To write a compound sentence, follow these rules.

1. **Make each part of the sentence a *complete thought.*** Include a **subject** (who or what the sentence is about) and a **verb** (what the subject does or is) in each part.

    Kay loved sports, and **she wanted** to be a sportswriter.

2. **Use the correct connecting word.**
    *   *and* for related ideas
    *   *or* for choices
    *   *so* for one idea that causes another
    *   *but* or *yet* for contrasting ideas

3. **Use a comma before the connecting word.**

    The newspaper needed a sports reporter**, so** the editor placed an ad.
    Kay applied for the job**, and** the editor called her for an interview.
    The editor recognized Kay's talent**, but** he didn't want to hire her.
    Kay's writing sample was good**, yet** she didn't have much experience.
    Kay could walk away**, or** she could speak up for herself.

Writing Complex Sentences

A complex sentence has two parts, an **independent clause** and a **dependent clause,** each with its own subject and verb:

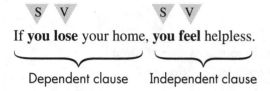

If **you lose** your home, **you feel** helpless.

Dependent clause   Independent clause

In the sentence above, the **dependent clause** begins with the connecting word *if*. Even though it has a subject and a verb, it does not make sense by itself. It cannot stand alone as a separate sentence. It depends on the independent clause to express a complete thought.

The second part of the example sentence is the **independent clause.** It is a complete thought, so it can stand alone. Here are some guidelines for writing complex sentences.

1. **Punctuation** You can put the dependent clause first or last in a sentence. If the dependent clause is first, put a **comma** after it. If the independent clause is first, do not use a comma.

   If you lose your home, you feel helpless.

   You feel helpless **if you lose your home.**

2. **Connecting words** A dependent clause begins with a dependent connecting word or phrase that indicates the relationship between the ideas in the two clauses. The chart below lists many of the common connecting words and phrases and the relationships they show. Notice that some words have more than one use.

Connecting Words and Phrases	Use to Show
after, as, as long as, as soon as, before, by the time, until, when, whenever, while	time relationships
as, because, in order that, since, so that	cause-and-effect relationships
if, in case, once, provided, unless	conditional relationships (conditions under which an event will occur)
although, even though, while	contrasting relationships

Correcting Sentence Fragments

A **complete sentence** contains a subject and a verb and expresses a complete thought. It can stand alone.

A **sentence fragment** does not express a complete thought. It cannot stand alone. Fragments make it hard for readers to understand what a writer means because the thoughts are incomplete. Here are some common types of fragments and ways to fix them.

1. **Fragment:** Before TV was invented.

   As you learned in Unit 2, this fragment is a **dependent clause.** It has a subject *(TV)* and a verb *(was invented),* but it is not a complete thought. It does not make sense by itself. To make a complete sentence, you can attach this fragment to an independent clause. Remember to add a comma after the dependent clause if it comes first:

   Before TV was invented, **people amused themselves in different ways.**
   People amused themselves in different ways before TV was invented.

2. **Fragment:** Televisions and radios two hundred years ago.

   This fragment has **no verb.** It does not make sense without one. To fix it, you can make the fragment into a complete sentence. Add a verb and any other words needed to make a complete thought:

   Televisions and radios **did not exist** two hundred years ago.
   People did not have televisions and radios two hundred years ago.

3. **Fragment:** Invented in the 20th century.

   This fragment has **no subject.** Depending on the subject, *invented* **may not be a complete verb.** To fix this kind of fragment, add a subject and a helping verb if needed to make it complete. You may need to add some other words, too.

   Television and computers were invented in the 20th century.
   Many useful things have been invented in the 20th century.
   Scientists invented **many useful things** in the 20th century.

4. **Fragment:** Thomas Edison. One of our greatest inventors.

   These fragments have **related ideas,** but they are **incomplete.** To fix them, you can combine them by adding a verb and any other necessary words.

   Thomas Edison **was** one of our greatest inventors.
   Thomas Edison, one of our greatest inventors, **was responsible for many changes.**

Correcting Run-on Sentences

Writing complete, separate sentences helps make your ideas easy to understand. If you run your sentences together, your ideas will not be clear. A **run-on sentence** has two or more independent clauses run together without a connecting word or correct punctuation. Look at this example:

Run-on sentence: They loved each other they thought marriage was risky.

Here are three ways to fix a run-on sentence like the one above:

1. **Divide the run-on into separate sentences.** Each sentence will have its own subject and verb, begin with a capital letter, and end with a period.

   They loved each other. They thought marriage was risky.

2. **Join the two independent clauses into a compound sentence.** Use a comma and a connecting word like *and, or, but, yet,* or *so.*

   They loved each other**, but** they thought marriage was risky.

3. **Create a complex sentence.** Use a connecting word like *when, after, because,* or *although.* Place the connecting word at the beginning of the dependent clause. Remember to use a comma if the dependent clause comes at the beginning of the sentence.

   Although they loved each other, they thought marriage was risky.

   They thought marriage was risky **even though they loved each other.**

Capitalization Rules

1. Capitalize the **first word of a sentence.**

2. Capitalize the **word** *I.*

3. Capitalize **people's titles** and **names.**
   Mr. Martin Pagano, Ms. Carla Raymundo, Mrs. Vista, Ted Beck,
   Dr. Albert Choi, Professor Sykes, Senator Feinstein

    Tip   Capitalize titles only when they are used with the person's name. Do not capitalize them when they appear alone.
   I like Professor Rashid. She is an excellent professor.

4. Capitalize **days of the week, holidays,** and **months.**
   Tuesday, Saturday, Thanksgiving, the Fourth of July, March, June

    Tip   Do not capitalize small words like *the, a, of,* or *and* unless they are at the beginning of a sentence.

5. Capitalize **geographical names** such as **cities, states, countries, bodies of water,** and **continents.**
   Detroit, Michigan, Japan, Pacific Ocean, Europe

6. Capitalize **names of organizations, institutions, companies,** and **brands.**
   the American Cancer Society, University of Delaware,
   Ford Motor Company, Kleenex

7. Capitalize **formal names of government bodies.**
   United States Congress, the Supreme Court, the Chicago City Council

8. Capitalize the **important words in titles of works** such as **books, magazines, newspapers, poems, songs, movies, plays, TV shows, etc.**
   The Prisoner of Second Avenue, Gone with the Wind, The Price Is Right

The Writing Process

The Writing Process is a series of stages that can help you create a good piece of writing. These stages are shown below.

1. Prewrite, or plan your writing.

    A. Think about your topic.

    B. List ideas about your topic.

    C. Organize your ideas.
- Decide which ideas you will use.
- Decide the order in which you will use them.
- Use an organizing method that works well for you.

2. Write a first draft.

    A. Use your ideas from stage 1. Also add, drop, or change ideas as you see fit.

    B. Write about your topic.
- Clearly state your main idea.
- Give specific details—facts, examples, reasons—to support your main idea.
- Group related ideas in paragraphs.
- Include an introduction and a conclusion.

3. Revise your first draft.

    A. Check that your first draft
- _____ includes your important ideas
- _____ develops your topic with supporting details
- _____ is clear and easy to understand
- _____ uses clue words to signal the organization of your ideas to your reader
- _____ has an introduction and a conclusion

    B. Make changes to improve your writing.
- Add, cross out, or move ideas.
- Reword ideas to make them clearer.
- Combine related ideas in sentences.

4. Edit your work.

    A. Check your draft for
- _____ complete sentences
- _____ correct spelling
- _____ correct punctuation
- _____ correct capitalization
- _____ correct usage and grammar

    B. Correct any mistakes you find. If you need help, use the Writing Skills Handbook on pages 171–175, or ask your instructor.

5. Recopy your draft.

    A. Write a final draft. Include all of your revising and editing changes.

    B. Compare your first and final drafts. Note improvements.

    C. Share your final draft with a classmate, a friend, or your instructor.